Cornelia Cecilia Eglantine (Ed.)

Sport in the Northern Territory

Cornelia Cecilia Eglantine (Ed.)

Sport in the Northern Territory

Northern, Territory, Sport, Tiwi, Islands, League, Football

TypPRESS

Imprint

Permission is granted to copy, distribute and/or modify this document under the terms of the GNU Free Documentation License, Version 1.2 or any later version published by the Free Software Foundation; with no Invariant Sections, with the Front-Cover Texts, and with the Back- Cover Texts. A copy of the license is included in the section entitled "GNU Free Documentation License".

All parts of this book are extracted from Wikipedia, the free encyclopedia (www.wikipedia.org).

You can get detailed informations about the authors of this collection of articles at the end of this book. The editors (Ed.) of this book are no authors. They have not modified or extended the original texts.

Pictures published in this book can be under different licences than the GNU Free Documentation License. You can get detailed informations about the authors and licences of pictures at the end of this book.

The content of this book was generated collaboratively by volunteers. Please be advised that nothing found here has necessarily been reviewed by people with the expertise required to provide you with complete, accurate or reliable information. Some information in this book maybe misleading or wrong. The Publisher does not guarantee the validity of the information found here. If you need specific advice (f.e. in fields of medical, legal, financial, or risk management questions) please contact a professional who is licensed or knowledgeable in that area.

Any brand names and product names mentioned in this book are subject to trademark, brand or patent protection and are trademarks or registered trademarks of their respective holders. The use of brand names, product names, common names, trade names, product descriptions etc. even without a particular marking in this works is in no way to be construed to mean that such names may be regarded as unrestricted in respect of trademark and brand protection legislation and could thus be used by anyone.

Cover image: www.ingimage.com
Concerning the licence of the cover image please contact ingimage.

Publisher:
TypPRESS is a trademark of
International Book Market Service Ltd., 17 Rue Meldrum, Beau Bassin, 1713-01 Mauritius
Email: info@bookmarketservice.com
Website: www.bookmarketservice.com

Published in 2012

Printed in: U.S.A., U.K., Germany. This book was not produced in Mauritius.

ISBN: 978-613-8-76194-5

Contents

Articles

Sport in the Northern Territory	1
Australian rules football in the Northern Territory	3
Tiwi Islands Football League	8
Tiwi Islands	11
Northern Territory Football League	19
AFL Northern Territory	22
Marrara Stadium	23
Traeger Park	24
Northern Territory Cricket	25
Rugby league in the Northern Territory	26
Northern Territory Rugby Union	28
V8 Supercars	29
Skycity Triple Crown	40
Darwin Football Stadium	42
Football Federation Northern Territory	43
North Queensland Fury F.C.	45
Sport in Australia	51
Northern Territory	66

References

Article Sources and Contributors	81
Image Sources, Licenses and Contributors	83

Sport in the Northern Territory

Many **sports** are played in the Northern Territory.

Australian rules football

The Tiwi Islands Football League is played in the Tiwi Islands. The Northern Territory Football League operates from Darwin. The Aboriginal All-Stars is also based in Darwin. The governing body for football in the territory is the AFL Northern Territory. Venues include the TIO Stadium in Darwin, and Traeger Park in Alice Springs.

Tiwi Islands Football League final

Cricket

Cricket is administered by Northern Territory Cricket.[1]

Rugby league

Rugby league is administered by the Northern Territory Rugby League. The territory has the highest participation rate per capita for Rugby League than any other state governing body in Australia. The National Rugby League has conducted numerous clinics and hosted regular pre-season matches in the territory since 1998. Local domestic competitions are based in Darwin, Alice Springs, Katherine and Gove. A combined Northern Territory team also participates in the Affiliated States Championship.

Rugby union

Rugby union is administered by the Northern Territory Rugby Union

Racing

The **Darwin Cup** culminating on the first Monday of August is a very popular horse race event for Darwin and draws large crowds every year to Fannie Bay Racecourse.

Motorsport

Darwin hosts a round of the V8 Supercar Championship Series every year, the Skycity Triple Crown, bringing thousands of motorsports fans to the Hidden Valley Raceway. The Hidden Valley Raceway facility also contains a drag strip as part of Hidden Valley Raceway's main straight, and a nearby Speedway, Northline Speedway, for short circuit dirt surface racing.

In the south of the Territory, Australia's biggest Off-Road Race, the Finke Desert Race is held over a long circuit which takes in the settlement of Aputula on the Finke River. The event is based out of Alice Springs.

Hidden Valley Raceway

Association football (soccer)

The Football Federation Northern Territory is the governing body for football (soccer) in the Northern Territory. The Territory is also separated into three (Northern, Central and Southern) zones which have their own zone councils which administer leagues locally running their own league and cup competitions.

The Darwin Football Stadium was officially opened on 28 July 2007 when it played host to an A-League Pre-Season Cup game between Perth Glory and Melbourne Victory. On 2 July 2009, A-League teams, Adelaide United FC and North Queensland Fury played a pre-season friendly at the stadium.[2]

Baseball

Baseball NT is the governing body of baseball within the Northern Territory. Baseball NT is governed by the Australian Baseball Federation.

Organised baseball is played in Darwin, Alice Springs and Katherine. Darwin has four clubs; Nightcliff Tigers, Palmerston Reds, Pints and Tracy Village Rebels. The East Darwin Beasts disbanded in 1986 and the South Darwin Rabbitohs disbanded in 2004.

For a brief history of baseball in Darwin, see Darwin baseball league and Northern Territory Buffalos. In Darwin, baseball is a dry-season sport, played between April and September each year.

Alice Springs has five teams; Bulls, Cubs, Demons, Panther and Redbacks

Events

Darwin also currently hosts state and international sporting events such as:
- Since 1991 Darwin has hosted the Arafura Games every two years.
- In July 2003, Darwin hosted its first international test cricket match between Australia and Bangladesh and then Australia and Sri Lanka in 2004.
- Melbourne's Western Bulldogs Australian Football League side plays one home game at Marrara Oval each year.
- The annual Camel Cup in Alice Springs.

References

[1] Northern Territory Cricket Official Site (http://www.ntcricket.com.au/)
[2] Reds Head For The Top End (http://au.fourfourtwo.com/news/103344,reds-head-for-the-top-end.aspx) *FourFourTwo Australia*, 15 May 2009

Australian rules football in the Northern Territory

Australian rules football in the Northern Territory

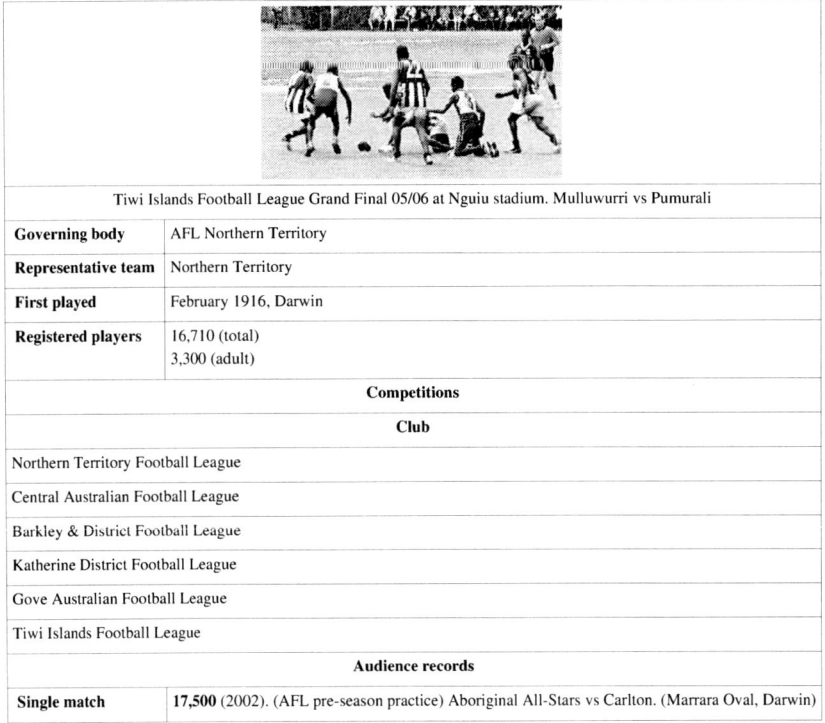

Tiwi Islands Football League Grand Final 05/06 at Nguiu stadium. Mulluwurri vs Pumurali

Governing body	AFL Northern Territory
Representative team	Northern Territory
First played	February 1916, Darwin
Registered players	16,710 (total) 3,300 (adult)
Competitions	
Club	
Northern Territory Football League	
Central Australian Football League	
Barkley & District Football League	
Katherine District Football League	
Gove Australian Football League	
Tiwi Islands Football League	
Audience records	
Single match	**17,500** (2002). (AFL pre-season practice) Aboriginal All-Stars vs Carlton. (Marrara Oval, Darwin)

Australian rules football in the Northern Territory has a history dating back to the 1910s and is the most popular sport in the territory, particularly with indigenous Australian communities in Darwin, Alice Springs and the Tiwi Islands.

7% of all Northern Territorians in 2007 participated in Australian rules football, the highest participation in Australia (and second worldwide only to Australian rules football in Nauru). The sport also produces more professional Australian rules footballers per capita in the Australian Football League than any other state or territory.

The Northern Territory is home to several representative teams, most notably the Aboriginal All-Stars, but also the **Northern Territory Thunder**, the Northern Territory Football Club (that plays in the QAFL) and the Flying Boomerangs and has a strong local competition, the Northern Territory Football League.

History

The first recorded match of Australian Football in Darwin was played in February 1916 on Darwin Town Oval.

The Northern Territory Football League chose to play in the Northern Territory's 'wet season', primarily due to hard playing surfaces during the 'dry season'. Most other leagues in Australia operate during the winter, but since the Territory does not have a winter, it is played at different times. The Wanderers Football Club were the founding members of the league in 1916.

John Pye and Andy Howley introduced Australian rules football to the Tiwi Islands

A football match being played in Darwin in 1943.

in 1941, which grew to become the most popular sport on the islands. The Tiwi Islands Football League is a strong competition which feeds players into the NTFL. Skills of the TIFL players are widely celebrated. The TIFL Grand Final is the largest event on the island and a major tourist drawcard.

In 1991, Marrara Stadium was increased in capacity, and became the new home for the NTFL and AFL matches.

In 1991, Darwin hosted the first Arafura Games, the first international competition to include the sport of Australian Rules, and local teams have competed against nations from around the world. The city has hosted the games since.

Since the late 1990s, the Aboriginal All-Stars have captured the imagination of indigenous Australians in the Northern Territory, and have gained a huge amount of support.

Recent History

Although the Territory would love to have a local team in the national competition, a small population and the lack of potential sponsorship means it is unlikely (but not impossible) that a team will be admitted to the Australian Football League at this time.

In 2002, a record crowd of 17,500 attended an AFL pre-season practice between the Aboriginal All-Stars and Carlton Football Club.

However, in a deal struck with the Northern Territory government, Melbourne based Western Bulldogs AFL side has played several *home* games a year at Marrara Stadium.

Central Australian Football League match at Traeger Park, Alice Springs.

In 2004, Alice Springs main ground Traeger Park was re-developed and has hosted several AFL exhibition matches.

In 2007, a representative side began in earnest a campaign to join a major league, the SANFL, WAFL or QAFL with the new team split between Alice Springs and Darwin. A decision was reached in late 2008, with the Northern

Territory Football Club, known as the Thunder, formed to field a team in the Queensland competition from the 2009 season onwards.

Representative Sides

The Northern Territory was represented in early Interstate matches in Australian rules football, before being incorporated into the QLD/NT and then Allies representative sides.

At Under 16 and Under 18 level, the territory fields teams in the national championships.

The Aboriginal All-Stars, a team composed of indigenous Australian players mostly from the AFL and all over the country, are based in Darwin. Darwin is also home of the Flying Boomerangs, the junior indigenous side, who play an annual series against South Africa.

The Northern Territory Football Club formed in 2009 to play in the QAFL competition.

Participation

In 2007, there were 3,300 senior players and a total of 16,710 participants in the Northern Territory[1]. The state has an overall participation rate in the sport per capita of 7%, making it the highest in the country. [2]

The Tiwi Islands is said to have the highest participation rate in Australia (35%) [3].

Audience

Attendance Record

- **17,500** (2002). (AFL pre-season practice) Aboriginal All-Stars vs Carlton. (Marrara Oval, Darwin)

Major Australian Rules Events in the Northern Territory

- Northern Territory Football League Grand Final
- Tiwi Islands Football League Grand Final
- Arafura Games (quadrennial)
- Australian Football League Premiership Season (Bulldogs 'home' games)

Great Northern Territory Footballers

Over the years, the Northern Territory has produced an amazing array of talent for elite leagues such as the Australian Football League and South Australian National Football League, including many indigenous Australian players. Greats include Maurice Rioli, Michael Long, Daryl White, Ronnie Burns, David Kantilla, Dean Rioli and Nathan Buckley.

Notable NT Players in the AFL

- Andrew McLeod
- Aaron Davey
- Joel Bowden
- Peter Burgoyne
- Matthew Whelan
- Jared Brennan
- Jason Roe
- Xavier Clarke
- Malcolm Lynch
- Anthony Corrie
- Trent Hentschel
- Richard Tambling
- Raphael Clarke
- Daniel Motlop
- Matthew Stokes
- Cyril Rioli
- Cameron Stokes
- Austin Wonaeamirri

Leagues

Open

State-wide Leagues

- Top End Australian Football Association

Darwin Metropolitan Leagues

- Northern Territory Football League

Regional Leagues

- Central Australian Football League
    - Northern Territory Champions League
- Barkley & District Football League
- Katherine District Football League
- Gove Australian Football League
- Tiwi Islands Football League

Women's

- Northern Territory Women's Aussie Rules Football Association Official Site [4]

Masters

- Masters Australian Football NT Official Site [5]

Principle Venues

- Marrara Stadium
- Traeger Park

See also

- AFL Northern Territory
- Northern Territory Football League

References

[1] More chase Sherrin than before - realfooty.com.au (http://realfooty.com.au/news/news/we-love-aussie-rules/2007/06/19/1182019117471.html)
[2] http://afl.com.au/cp2/c2/webi/article/205058bu.pdf
[3] http://www.theage.com.au/news/northern-territory/even-a-cyclone-cant-stop-the-footy/2005/03/19/1111086063413.html
[4] http://web.archive.org/web/20091027043205/http://geocities.com/womensfootball/ntwarfa/
[5] http://www.sportingpulse.com.au/club_info.cgi?clubID=24971&club=Northern%20Territory&client=%40MAF%20Carnival%202005%40981%40%40%40%40%40%40%404%40%40%40

- AFL Northern Territory
- Australian Football League

External links

- NT Team of the Century from Full Points Footy (http://www.fullpointsfooty.net/northern_territory.htm)
- Even a Cyclone can't stop the footy (http://www.theage.com.au/news/northern-territory/even-a-cyclone-cant-stop-the-footy/2005/03/19/1111086063413.html)

Tiwi Islands Football League

Current season or competition: 2010-11 Wet Season	
Sport	Australian rules football
Founded	1969
No. of teams	8
Country(ies)	Australia
Most recent champion(s)	Imalu Football Club (Tigers)
Most titles	Imalu Football Club (16)Draw in 85/86 Tapalinga won replay
TV partner(s)	ABC1

The **Tiwi Islands Football League** is an Australian rules football competition in the Tiwi Islands, Northern Territory, Australia. Australian Rules football is the most popular sport on the Tiwi Islands. The Grand Final of the TIFL is broadcast each year on ABC Northern and more recently, nationally on ABC2 and ABC1.

Tiwi football

The Tiwi Islands Grand Final is an event held in March each year that attracts up to 3,000 spectators and is a tourist attraction for the Northern Territory. The Tiwi Australian Football League has 900 participants out of a community of about 2600, the highest football participation rate in Australia (35%).
[1] Tiwi footballers are renknowned for exquisite *one touch* skills. Many of the players have a preference for participating barefoot. Many of the male players also play for the St Marys Football Club in Darwin's Northern Territory Football League.

Action from the 2005 TIFL Grand Final between Pumarali (red and white) and Muluwurri (black and white).

Results

Wet Season Grand Final

1969/70 Tapalinga def. Pumaralli (scores not known)
1970/71 Irrimaru 15.6 (96) def. Pumaralli 9.14 (68)
1972/73 Imalu def. Tapalinga by 55 points (scores not known)
1973/74 Imalu 12.8 (80) def. Pumaralli 8.5 (53)
1974/75 Tuyu 11.8 (74) def. Imalu 10.13 (73)
1975/76 Pumaralli 13.16 (94) def. Tuyu 8.12 (60)
1976/77 Tapalinga 12.6 (78) def. Pumaralli 10.9 (69)

1977/78 Pumaralli 14.15 (99) def. Imalu 10.9 (69)
1978/79 Imalu 25.15 (165) def. Tapalinga 2.3 (15)
1979/80 Pumaralli 10.16 (76) def. Taracumbi 7.10 (52)
1980/81 Imalu 12.12 (84) def. Pumaralli 12.7 (79)
1981/82 Imalu 20.8 (128) def. Tapalinga 8.18 (66)
1982/83 Tapalinga 18.17 (125) def. Pumaralli 19.5 (119)
1983/84 Imalu 16.13 (109) def. Tapalinga 15.16 (106)
1984/85 Imalu 14.10 (94) def. Irrimaru 7.13 (55)
1985/86 Imalu 21.3 (129) v Tapalinga 19.15 (129) DRAW
1985/86 Tapalinga 24.12 (156) def. Imalu 22.3 (135) REPLAY
1986/87 Tapalinga 22.7 (139) def. Pumaralli 16.13 (109)
1987/88 Tapalinga 18.13 (121) def. Imalu 14.14 (98)
1988/89 Imalu 18.9 (117) def. Taracumbi 11.17 (83)
1989/90 Imalu 23.22 (160) def. Taracumbi 14.11 (95)
1990/91 Tapalinga 14.9 (93) def. Imalu 12.8 (80)
1991/92 Imalu 19.5 (119) def. Tuyu 12.10 (82)
1992/93 Imalu 15.8 (98) def. Irrimaru 9.11 (65)
1993/94 Imalu 22.25 (157) def. Tuyu 14.5 (89)
1994/95 Tuyu 15.12 (102) def. Irrimaru 11.11 (77)
1995/96 Imalu 17.9 (111) def. Tuyu 10.12 (72)
1996/97 Irrimaru 13.6 (84) def. Imalu 12.6 (78)
1997/98 Tapalinga 17.7 (109) def. Pumaralli 11.5 (71)
1998/99 Imalu 9.8 (62) def. Ranku 3.6 (24)
1999/00 Pumarrali 8.6 (54) def. Tuyu 6.12 (48)
2000/01 Ranku 12.7 (79) def. Taracumbi 9.7 (61)
2001/02 Tuyu 7.8 (50) def. Tapalinga 6.6 (42)
2002/03 Pumaralli 11.10 (76) def. Muluwurri 7.10 (52)
2003/04 Tapalinga 10.10 (70) def. Imalu 9.6 (60)
2004/05 Tuyu 12.9 (81) def. Muluwurri 10.3 (63)
2005/06 Pumaralli 7.7 (49) def. Muluwurri 6.8 (44)
2006/07 Muluwurri 25.6 (156) def. Imalu 12.4 (76)
2007/08 Imalu 12.9 (81) def. Tapalinga 10.8 (68)
2008/09 Tapalinga 12.9 (81) def. Imalu 11.7 (73) [2]
2009/10 Tapalinga 9.15 (69) def. Imalu 4.6 (30) [3]
2010/11 Imalu 13.10 (88) def. Ranku 6.7 (43) [4]

Clubs

- Imalu Football Club (Tigers)
- Walama Football Club (Bulldogs (formerly Irrimaru Football Club)
- Pumarali Football Club (Thunder & Lightning)
- Tapalinga Football Club (Superstars)
- Muluwurri Magpies (Magpie Geese - formerly Taracumbi Football Club)
- Tuyu Football Club (Buffaloes)
- Ranku Football Club (Eagles)
- Melville Island Roos Football Club (Kangaroos)

Former clubs
- Warankuwu Football Club
- Nguiu Football Club

History

Br. John Pye and Br. Andy Howley introduced Australian rules football to Bathurst and Melville islands in 1941.

The locals quickly took to the game and the first dedicated ground was built in 1942.

In 1944 the first games consisting of a full complement of 18 players and matches according to the rule book were played.

In 1954, the St Mary's Football Club began enlisting Tiwi servicemen, and in the following year with the assistance of a majority of Tiwi players won the NTFL premiership.

In the 1960s, the most talented export of the TIFL, David Kantilla had a successful career in the NTFL, which reached a peak when he later became a professional player in the South Adelaide Football Club (SANFL) premiership ruckman, and winning leading goal kicking and Best and Fairest awards at the club. The league's top goalkicking award was later named after him.

The 1969/1970 Wet Season saw the first season of the TIFL, with 5 teams competing: Pumarali, Tapalinga, Imalu, Tuyu and Irrimaru.

In 1982, Tiwi Maurice Rioli won the Norm Smith Medal for the Richmond Football Club, becoming one of the first Tiwis to succeed in the VFL/AFL. Michael Long was later to do the same in 1993. Adam Kerinaiua played 3 games for the Brisbane Bears in 1992. Malcolm Lynch is a more recent product of the Tiwi Islands playing the AFL. Although these players were not from the TIFL, the success of these players in the elite Australian competition did much to boost the popularity of Australian Rules amongst the local Tiwi Islanders.

In 2006, it was announced that a Tiwi Islands Football Club would join the Northern Territory Football League initially known as the "Super Tiwis". [5] The team began 2006 season as the "Tiwi Bombers".[6]

See also
- AFL Northern Territory
- Northern Territory Football League
- Australian rules football in the Northern Territory

References

[1] Even a cyclone can't stop the footy (http://www.theage.com.au/news/northern-territory/even-a-cyclone-cant-stop-the-footy/2005/03/19/1111086063413.html)
[2] ABC1 Telecast 22 March 2009
[3] ABC1 Telecast 14 March 2010
[4] ABC1 Telecast 27 March 2011
[5] Northern Territory News (http://ntnews.news.com.au/common/story_page/0,7034,18629572%5E13569,00.html)
[6] Tiwis take a leap in their hopes for the side (http://www.realfooty.theage.com.au/realfooty/articles/2006/10/12/1160246263971.html)

External links

- Aboriginal Football list of TIFL Grand Final scores and winners of Brother John Pye Award, Ted Whitten Award, David Kantilla Award and Mitch Lee Award (http://sportingpulse.com/assoc_page.cgi?c=1-5545-0-0-0&sID=75919)
- Tiwi Local Government Pages (http://www.tilg.nt.gov.au/home/tiwi_links/tiwi_islands_football_league)
- Even a cyclone can't stop the footy (http://www.theage.com.au/news/northern-territory/even-a-cyclone-cant-stop-the-footy/2005/03/19/1111086063413.html)
- Interview with Brother John Pye - founder of Tiwi Footy (http://www.abc.net.au/stateline/nt/content/2006/s1600507.htm)

Tiwi Islands

The **Tiwi Islands** are part of Australia's Northern Territory, north of Darwin where the Arafura Sea joins the Timor Sea. They comprise Melville Island and Bathurst Island, with a combined area of 8320 square kilometres (3212 sq mi).

Inhabited before European settlement by the Tiwi indigenous Australians, there are approximately 2500 people on the islands.

The Tiwi Land Council is one of four in the Northern Territory. It is a representative body with statutory authority under the Aboriginal Land Rights (Northern Territory) Act 1976 and has responsibilities under the Native Title Act 1993 and the Pastoral Land Act 1992.

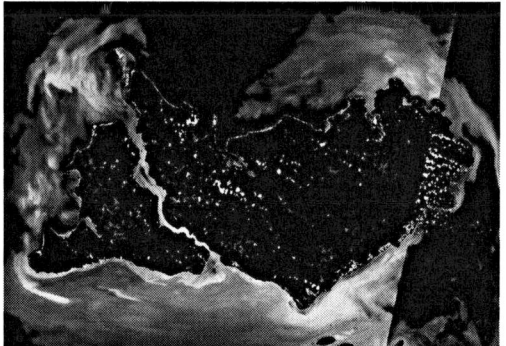

Landsat 7 imagery of the Tiwi Islands.

Geography and population

The Tiwi Islands lie 80km to the north of Australia's Northern Territory in the Arafura Sea, and are part of the Northern Territory[1]. Bathurst Island is the fifth-largest island of Australia and accessible by sea or air.[2] Melville Island is Australia's second largest island (after Tasmania).[3]

The islands are separated by Apsley Strait, which connects Saint Asaph Bay in the north and Shoal Bay in the south, and is between 550 metres and 5 km wide, 62 km long. At the mouth of Shoal Bay is Buchanan Island, with an area of about 3 km². A car ferry at the narrowest point provides a quick connection between the two islands.

Tiwi Islands Car Ferry, 2011

They are inhabited by the Tiwi people, as they have been since before European settlement in Australia. The Tiwi are an Indigenous Australian people, culturally and linguistically distinct from those of Arnhem Land on the mainland just across the water. They number around 2500.[4] In 2006 the total population of the islands was 2129, of whom 91.3% were Aboriginal.[5] Most residents speak Tiwi as their first language and English as a second language.[6] Most of the population live in Wurrumiyanga (known as Nguiu until 2010) on Bathurst Island, and Pirlangimpi (also known as Garden Point) and Milikapiti (also known as Snake Bay) on Melville Island. Wurrumiyanga has a population of nearly 1500, the other two centres around 450 each.[7]

Traditional burial poles, Tiwi Islands, 2005.

There are other smaller settlements, including Wurankuwu (Ranku) Community on western Bathurst Island.[8]

History

Indigenous Australians have occupied the Tiwi Islands for centuries, with creation stories suggesting they were present at least 7000 years before present.[9]

Tiwi islanders are believed to have had contact with Macassan traders,[10] and the first historical record of contact between Indigenous islanders and western explorers was with the Dutch 'under the command of Commander Maarten van Delft who took three ships into Shark Bay on Melville Island and landed on 30 April 1705'.[9] There were other visits by explorers and navigators in the seventeenth, eighteenth and nineteenth centuries, including by Dutchman Pieter Pieterszoon, Frenchman Nicholas Baudin and Briton Philip Parker King.[11]

The first European settlement on the Islands was at Fort Dundas, near present-day Pirlangimpi on Melville Island. Established in September 1824, this was the first British settlement in northern Australia, but owing in part to the hostility of the Indigenous population it lasted only five years, being abandoned in 1829.[11] As "the first attempted European and military settlement anywhere in northern Australia", the site is on Australia's Register of the National Estate.[12]

A Catholic mission was established by Francis Xavier Gsell in 1911,[9] [10] and the islands were proclaimed an Aboriginal Reserve in 1912. A timber church built in the 1930s is a prominent landmark in Wurrumiyanga.[10] The catholic mission thrived until 1972 and provided invaluable education to the Tiwi people. This including the provision of agricultural skills and the Tiwi people successfully sold crops such as bananas to the main land. With self-determination declared in 1972, the mission activities effectively ceased. However, a continuing catholic presence of Brothers, Sisters and Priests was requested by the Tiwi people of Nguiu to assist with education and health services.

Nguiu Catholic church in 2005

Control of the islands was transferred to the Indigenous traditional owners through the Tiwi Aboriginal Land Trust, and the Tiwi Land Council that was founded in 1978.[9] The Tiwi Islands Local Government Area was established in 2001, when the previous community government councils in the three main communities of Wurrumiyanga (Bathurst Island), Pirlangimpi and Milikapiti (Melville Island) were amalgamated with the Wurankuwu Aboriginal Corporation to form a single local government.[13] The Tiwi Islands Local Government was replaced in 2008 by the Tiwi Islands Shire Council as part of a Northern Territory-wide restructuring of local government.[14]

Politics and administration

The Tiwi Islands are part of the Federal electorate of Lingiari,[15] for which the current member is Warren Snowdon.[16] The islands are within the Northern Territory electorate of Arafura. The current Member for Arafura is Marion Scrymgour.[17]

The administration of the Islands is divided between the local Tiwi Islands Shire Council, and the Indigenous landholder representative organisation, the Tiwi Land Council. Representatives on the Shire Council are elected from four wards, and include 11 councillors;[4]

1. Milikapiti Ward (northeast Melville Island, largest)
2. Nguiu Ward (south Bathurst Island, Buchanan Island)
3. Pirlangimpi Ward (west and southwest Melville Island)
4. Wurankuwu Ward (north Bathurst Island)

In 2005–06, the operating budget of the Tiwi Islands Shire Council was A$27.7 million.[18]

Culture

Indigenous Art

The creation of Indigenous Australian art is an important part of Tiwi Island culture and its economy. There are three Indigenous art centres on the islands: Tiwi Design, Munupi Arts & Crafts, and Jilamara Arts and Craft,[19] and these collaborate through a cooperative venture, Tiwi Art.[20] Apart from Tiwi Art network there are two independent operations: fabric design, printing and clothing business Bima Wear,[21] operated by Indigenous women since 1969, and Ngaruwanajirri, also known as 'The Keeping Place'.

Tiwi artists who have held international exhibitions or whose works are held in major Australian collections include Donna Burak,[22] Jean Baptiste Apuatimi,[23] and Fiona Puruntatameri.[24]

A lot of wood carvings of birds are made by Tiwi people. Some of these are displayed in the Mission Heritage Gallery on Bathurst Island. The carvings represent various birds from Tiwi mythology, which have various meanings. Certain birds tell the Tiwi people about approaching monsoonal rains whilst others warn of impending cyclones. Others, depending on the totem of the

Picture of Tiwi Island decorated carvings, 2005.

people, alert the Tiwi people that someone has died in a particular clan. There are others that represent ancestral beings who were, according to mythology, changed into birds. Carved birds are sometimes at the top of pukumani poles, which are placed at sacred burial sites.

The Tiwi People also create many of their designs on fabric. The main method uses wax to resist dying similarly to Indonesian batik prints. Various fabrics are used ranging from sturdy, woven cotton to delicate silks, from which they create silk scarves.

Tiwi Island bird carvings, 2011

The creation of their artwork is usually a social activity and consists of groups of people sitting together and talking whist they work in a relaxed fashion. Often these grouping are segregated by gender.

Australian Rules Football

Australian rules football is the most popular sport on the Tiwi Islands, and was introduced in 1941 by missionary John Pye.[25] There has been a Tiwi Islands Football League competition since 1969.[26]

Ceiling of a Tiwi Island art gallery and studio, 2011

A Tiwi Islands Aussie Rules game.

The Tiwi Islands Football League Grand Final is held in March each year and attracts up to 3,000 spectators. The Tiwi Australian Football League has 900 participants out of a community of about 2600, the highest football participation rate in Australia (35%).[27]

Tiwi footballers are renowned for exquisite *one touch* skills. Many of the players have a preference for playing barefoot. Many of the male players also play for the St Mary's Football Club in Darwin, which was formed specifically to allow Tiwi soldiers in the 1950s to play in the Northern Territory Football League.

The Tiwi Islands Football Club (Tiwi Bombers) fielded a team in the Northern Territory Football League from the 2006/07 season.

Notable footballers from the Tiwi Islands include Ronnie Burns,[28] Maurice Rioli,[29] Cyril Rioli,[29] Dean Rioli, Michael Long,[28] Malcolm Lynch, Austin Wonaeamirri[30] and David Kantilla.[31]

The Tiwi Islands Football Club was the subject of a series on ABC's Message Stick in 2009, called *In A League of Their Own*.[32]

Cricket

As reported in The Weekend Australian, in 2010 Australian Cricketers led by Mathew Hayden raised $200,000 for cricket development in the Tiwi Islands. With former internationals Allan Border, Michael Kasprowicz and Andy Bichel, the match between Hayden XI and Border XI had a turnout of 1000 people, nearly half the islands' population.[33]

Transport

A commercial flight operator, Fly Tiwi, connects both islands to each other and to Darwin. Formed as an association between Hardy Aviation and the Tiwi Land Council, Fly Tiwi has daily flights to all three communities on the islands.[34]

The *Arafura Pearl* ferry connects Wurrumiyanga and Darwin, and makes the two hour trip each way on three days a week.[35]

In 2008, local government maintained 925 kilometres of roads on the islands.[18]

Environment, conservation and land use

The islands' climatic and geographical extremity means that they have distinctive vegetation and special conservation values:

> because of their isolation and because they have extremely high rainfall, the Tiwi Islands support many species not recorded elsewhere in the Northern Territory (or in the world), and some range-restricted species. The Tiwi Islands contain the Territory's best-developed (tallest and with greatest basal area) eucalypt forests and an unusually high density and extent of rainforests.[2]

Climate

The Tiwi Islands have a tropical monsoonal climate, with 2000 mm of rainfall on northern Bathurst Island and 1200 to 1400 mm on eastern Melville Island.[36] The wet season from November to April brings the islands highest rainfall in the Northern Territory.[37] The Tiwi people describe three distinct seasons: the dry (season of smoke), the build up (high humidity and cicadas songs) and the wet (storms) The seasons frame the lifestyle of the Tiwi people, dictating the food sources available and their ceremonial activities[38].

Flora and fauna

The islands have been isolated from the Australian mainland since the last ice age. They are covered mainly with eucalypt forest on a gently sloping lateritic plateau. The extensive open forest, open woodlands and riparian vegetation are dominated by Darwin Stringybarks, Woollybutts, and Cajuputs. There are small patches of rainforest occurring in association with perennial freshwater springs, and mangroves occupying the numerous inlets.[37]

There is a range of threatened and endemic species on the Tiwi Islands. Thirty-eight threatened species have been recorded, and a number of plants and invertebrates are found nowhere else, including eight plant species and some land snails and dragonflies.[39] Threatened mammals include Brush-Tailed Rabbit Rats, Northern Brush-tailed Phascogales, False Water Rats and Carpentarian Dunnarts.[37] The islands host the world's largest breeding colony of Crested Terns and a large population of the vulnerable olive ridley turtle;[39] a sea turtle conservation program commenced on the islands in 2007.[39] The seas and estuaries around the islands are home to several species of shark and saltwater crocodiles.

Important Bird Area

The islands have been identified as an Important Bird Area (IBA) by BirdLife International because they support relatively high densities of Red Goshawks, Partridge Pigeons and Bush Stone-curlews, as well as up to 12,000 (over 1% of the world population) Great Knots. Other birds for which the Tiwi Island populations are globally significant include Chestnut Rails, Beach Stone-curlews Northern Rosellas, Varied Lorikeets, Rainbow Pittas, Silver-crowned Friarbirds, White-gaped, Yellow-tinted and Bar-breasted Honeyeaters, Canary White-eyes and Masked Finches.[40] The birds have a high level of endemism at the subspecific level; the Tiwi Masked Owl (*Tyto novaehollandiae melvillensis*) is considered Endangered and the Tiwi Hooded Robin (*Melanodryas cucullata melvillensis*) is at least endangered and may be extinct.[37]

Forestry and mining

Forest products are an important part of the Tiwi Islands economy, but the sector has had a chequered history. Forestry dates back to 1898, with plantations being trialled from the 1950s and 1960s.[41] [42] A native softwood enterprise was established in the mid-1980s, as a partnership between the private sector and the Land Council; however by the mid-1990s, the Land Council was winding the venture down, noting that its investor partner had "various tax driven ambitions which are growingly incompatible with our own employment and sustainable production goals".[43] Despite the setback, it was still considered that forestry was likely to be crucial to the Tiwi economy,[44] and in 2001 the Land Council and Australian Plantations Group commenced a major expansion of *Acacia mangium* plantations to supply woodchips.[45] The operations of Australian Plantations Group (later named Sylvatech) were purchased by Great Southern Group in 2005.[46] In 2006, the operations were reported to be "the largest native-forest clearing project in northern Australia".[47] In September 2007 the Northern Territory Government investigated claims that the company had breached environmental laws,[48] with financial penalties being imposed by the Federal environment department in 2008.[47] Much of the cleared land is used for cattle or monoculture plantations, which the timber company has maintained are an important source of local jobs.[49] Great Southern Plantations collapsed in early 2009, and the Tiwi Land Council has been examining options for future management of the plantations.[50]

The islands have mineral sands on both Melville Island's north coast and the western coast of Bathurst Island.[44] In 2005, Matilda Minerals developed a proposal for mining on the islands, which was assessed and approved in 2006.[51] In 2007 sand mining produced the first shipments of zircon and rutile for export to China.[52] A 7,800 tonne shipment was made in June 2007,[53] with a further 5,000 tonnes shipped later that year.[52] Matilda Minerals planned to conduct mining for four years,[52] however in August 2008 its Tiwi operations were halted, and in October it was placed in administration.[54] [55]

See also

- Hector (storm)

References

[1] http://www.about-australia.com/northern-territory/darwin/destinations/bathurst-island/
[2] "Sites of Conservation Significance: Tiwi Islands" (http://nt.gov.au/nreta/environment/conservation/pdf/09_tiwi.pdf). Northern Territory Department of Natural Resources, Environment, the Arts and Sport. . Retrieved 2009-05-27.
[3] "Education:geoscience basics: islands" (http://www.ga.gov.au/education/geoscience-basics/landforms/islands.jsp). Geoscience Australia. 2009. . Retrieved 2009-05-27.
[4] Tiwi Islands Shire Council "Bushtel: Northern Territory: Northern Region: Tiwi Shire" (http://www.bushtel.nt.gov.au/northern_territory/region1/shire_id1). Government of the Northern Territory. 2007. Tiwi Islands Shire Council. Retrieved 2009-05-21.
[5] "4705.0 Population Distribution, Aboriginal and Torres Strait Islander Australians, 2006" (http://www.abs.gov.au/AUSSTATS/abs@.nsf/DetailsPage/4705.02006?OpenDocument). Australian Bureau of Statistics. 2007-08-15. . Retrieved 2009-05-27.
[6] Barker, Anne (2003-09-26). "Tiwi Islands School Wins English Literacy Award" (http://www.abc.net.au/stateline/nt/content/2003/s954762.htm). *ABC Stateline*. . Retrieved 2009-05-27.

[7] "Tiwi Islands Shire Council Business Plan 2008-2009" (http://www.localgovernment.nt.gov.au/__data/assets/pdf_file/0003/31962/TIS_Business_Plan_-_Main_Report2.pdf). Tiwi Islands Shire Council. July 2008. . Retrieved 2009-05-27.

[8] "Welcome to the Wurankuwu Community Online Information Directory" (http://www.rankustore.com/). Ranku Store. . Retrieved 2009-05-27.

[9] "Tiwi Land Council: History" (http://www.tiwilandcouncil.net.au/AboutUs/About_us.htm). Tiwi Land Council. 2008. . Retrieved 2008-08-27.

[10] Squires, Nick (2005-07-16). "Aborigines' island life" (http://news.bbc.co.uk/1/hi/programmes/from_our_own_correspondent/4686945.stm). BBC News. . Retrieved 2009-05-27.

[11] Forrest, Peter (1995). *The Tiwi Meet the Dutch: The First European Contacts* (http://www.tiwilandcouncil.net.au/Publications/Dutchtiwistory.pdf). Tiwi Land Council. .

[12] "Fort Dundas, Pularumpi, NT, Australia (entry AHD18163)" (http://www.environment.gov.au/cgi-bin/ahdb/search.pl?mode=place_detail;place_id=18163). *Australian Heritage Database*. Department of Sustainability, Environment, Water, Population and Communities. 1993-06-22. . Retrieved 2009-06-30.

[13] Tiwi Islands Local Government (July 2002). "Tiwi Islands Local Government, Submission to Inquiry into Local Government and Cost Shifting" (http://www.aph.gov.au/house/committee/efpa/localgovt/submissions/sub50.pdf). House of Representatives Standing Committee on Economics, Finance and Public Administration. . Retrieved 2009-05-27.

[14] Elliot McAdam (Minister for Local Government) (2007-08-22). "Local Government Changes Introduced" (http://newsroom.nt.gov.au/index.cfm?fuseaction=printRelease&ID=2879). . Retrieved 2009-05-27.

[15] "Map of Commonwealth Electoral Division of Lingiari" (http://www.aec.gov.au/pdf/profiles/l/lingiari.pdf). Australian Electoral Commission. 2007. . Retrieved 2009-05-21.

[16] "The Hon Warren Snowdon MP" (http://www.aph.gov.au/house/members/member.asp?id=IJ4). Parliament of Australia. . Retrieved 2009-05-27.

[17] "Electorate of Arafura: Profile" (http://notes.nt.gov.au/nteo/Electorl.nsf/94150a183d04f75f692564e2000ed605/209bd2efe05dc8ba6925693600061c16?OpenDocument). Northern Territory Electoral Commission. . Retrieved 2009-05-27.

[18] Northern Territory Department of Local Government and Housing (August 2008). "Local Government Regional Management Plan - Northern Region" (http://www.localgovernment.nt.gov.au/__data/assets/pdf_file/0016/41506/NORTHERN_REGION_RMP_Aug_08.pdf). . Retrieved 2009-09-07.

[19] "A Guide to Aboriginal Art and the Aboriginal Owned Art Centres of the Kimberley and Top End" (http://www.ankaaa.org.au/ANKAAA_ArtGuideBrochure.pdf). Association of Northern, Kimberley and Arnhem Aboriginal Artists. 2008. . Retrieved 2009-05-27.

[20] "Tiwi Art" (http://www.tiwiart.com/). . Retrieved 2009-05-27.

[21] "Bima Wear" (http://www.bimawear.com/). . Retrieved 2009-07-13.

[22] "ANKAAA biography: Donna Burak – Tiwi Region" (http://www.ankaaa.org.au/Committee_profile/Donna_burak.html). Association of Northern, Kimberley and Arnhem Aboriginal Artists. . Retrieved 2009-05-27.

[23] "Tiwi Art - upcoming exhibitions" (http://www.tiwiart.com/exhibitions.asp?iToDisplay=2). Tiwi Art. . Retrieved 2009-05-27.

[24] "Aboriginal & Torres Strait Islander Art Collection: Snapper" (http://artsearch.nga.gov.au/Detail.cfm?IRN=2952&PICTAUS=TRUE). National Gallery of Australia. . Retrieved 2009-05-27.

[25] "Tiwi Islands Grand Final" (http://www.abc.net.au/stateline/nt/content/2006/s1600507.htm). *Stateline* (Australian Broadcasting Corporation). 2006-03-24. . Retrieved 2008-08-15.

[26] "Tiwi Islands Football League: 1969 - 2008" (http://sportingpulse.com/assoc_page.cgi?c=1-5545-0-0-0&sID=75919). 2008. . Retrieved 2009-05-27.

[27] "Even a cyclone can't stop the footy" (http://www.theage.com.au/news/northern-territory/even-a-cyclone-cant-stop-the-footy/2005/03/19/1111086063413.html). *The Sun-Herald*. 2005-03-20. . Retrieved 2006-05-14.

[28] Roffey, Chelsea (2009-05-21). "The Tiwi effect" (http://www.afl.com.au/tabid/208/default.aspx?newsid=77217). *AFL BigPond*. . Retrieved 2009-06-29.

[29] McFarlane, Glenn (2008-08-31). "Maurice: Cyril may be best Rioli yet" (http://www.news.com.au/heraldsun/sport/afl/story/0,26576,24269334-19767,00.html). *Herald Sun*. . Retrieved 2009-05-27.

[30] Burgan, Matt (2008-05-22). "Q&A with Austin Wonaeamirri" (http://www.melbournefc.com.au/tabid/7415/Default.aspx?newsid=60016). *Melbourne Football Club*. . Retrieved 2009-05-27.

[31] "St Mary's F.C. - David Kantilla" (http://stmarysfc0.tripod.com/id59.html). . Retrieved 2009-05-27.

[32] "In A League of Their Own" (http://inaleagueoftheirown.com.au/). 2009. . Retrieved 2009-05-21.

[33] http://blogs.cricinfo.com/thebuzz/

[34] "About Fly Tiwi" (http://www.flytiwi.com.au/data/aboutus.php). Fly Tiwi. . Retrieved 2009-06-30.

[35] "Arafura Pearl timetable" (http://www.seacat.com.au/ArafuraPearl.htm). Sea-cat ferries and charters. . Retrieved 2009-06-30.

[36] "Tiwi Islands Regional Natural Resource Management Strategy" (http://www.tiwilandcouncil.net.au/Land/PDF_NRMS/Tiwi_physical_profile.pdf). Tiwi Land Council. . Retrieved 2009-05-27.

[37] BirdLife International. (2011). Important Bird Areas factsheet: Tiwi Islands. Downloaded from http://www.birdlife.org on 2011-11-06.

[38] http://www.tiwiart.com/tiwi_islands/item/9

[39] "Sea Turtle Conservation and Education on the Tiwi Islands" (http://www.environment.gov.au/coasts/publications/pubs/tiwi-turtle-conservation.pdf). Department of the Environment and Water Resources, Commonwealth of Australia. 2007. . Retrieved

2008-08-15.
[40] "IBA: Tiwi Islands" (http://www.birdata.com.au/iba.vm). *Birdata*. Birds Australia. . Retrieved 2011-11-06.
[41] Tiwi Land Council (March 2009). "Tiwi Land Council Submission to the Inquiry into Mining and Forestry on the Tiwi Islands" (https:// senate.aph.gov.au/submissions/comittees/viewdocument.aspx?id=6409d1ea-3d42-4a44-912f-f26fd6034b24). Senate Environment, Communications and the Arts References Committee. . Retrieved 2009-05-27.
[42] CSIRO (March 2009). "CSIRO Submission to the Inquiry into Mining and Forestry on the Tiwi Islands" (https://senate.aph.gov.au/ submissions/comittees/viewdocument.aspx?id=80167139-c85f-49a9-b6e0-534ba2cedb19). Senate Environment, Communications and the Arts References Committee. . Retrieved 2009-05-27.
[43] Tiwi Land Council (November 1996). *Tiwi Islands Region Economic Development Strategy*. Winnellie, NT: Tiwi Land Council.
[44] Tiwi Land Council (2004). *Tiwi Islands Regional Natural Resource Management Strategy*. Winnellie, NT: Tiwi Land Council.
[45] Australian Plantation Group Pty Ltd; Tiwi Land Council (2001-03-30). *Australian Plantation Group Pty Ltd/Forestry/Melville Island/NT/Hardwood Plantation: Invitation for public comment* (http://www.environment.gov.au/cgi-bin/epbc/epbc_ap. pl?name=current_referral_detail&proposal_id=330). Canberra: Department of Environment, Water, Heritage and the Arts.
[46] Great Southern Limited (2005). *Annual Report 2005* (http://www.great-southern.com.au/Annual_Reports.aspx). .
[47] Wilkinson, Marian (2008-10-16). "Forest firm told to pay $2m for damaging islands" (http://www.smh.com.au/news/environment/ forest-firm-told-to-pay-2m-for-damaging-islands/2008/10/15/1223750129823.html). *Sydney Morning Herald*. . Retrieved 2009-06-29.
[48] "Woodchip plantation breached environmental conditions: report" (http://www.abc.net.au/news/stories/2007/09/16/2034000.htm). *ABC News* (Australian Broadcasting Corporation). 2007-09-16. . Retrieved 2008-08-15.
[49] "Land clearing threatens Tiwi Islands" (http://www.smh.com.au/news/National/Land-clearing-threatens-Tiwi-islands/2007/09/19/ 1189881579181.html). *The Sydney Morning Herald* (Fairfax Ltd). 2007-09-17. . Retrieved 2008-08-15.
[50] "$80 million needed for Tiwi plantations: council" (http://www.abc.net.au/news/stories/2009/07/16/2627980.htm). *ABC News* (Australian Broadcasting Corporation). 2009-07-16. . Retrieved 2009-07-18.
[51] Northern Territory Government Environmental Protection Agency Program (May 2006). *Andranangoo Creek West and Lethbridge Bay West Mineral Sands Mining Project: Environmental Assessment Report and Recommendations* (http://www.nt.gov.au/nreta/environment/ assessment/register/matildaminerals/pdf/MatildaAssessmentReport-Final.pdf). Darwin, NT: Department of Natural Resources, Environment and the Arts. .
[52] "Matilda's first shipment waltzes away" (http://www.astronchem.com/english/investors/20070803_Media Clip - Astron.pdf). Astron Ltd. 2007-08-03. . Retrieved 2009-06-29.
[53] "Matilda sends first sands from Tiwi Islands" (http://www.lloydslistdcn.com.au/archive/2007/jun/21/ matilda-sends-first-sands-from-tiwi-islands). *Lloyd's List Daily Commercial News* (Informa Australia Pty Ltd). 2007-06-21. . Retrieved 2009-06-29.
[54] "Matilda Minerals Limited" (http://www.ferrierhodgson.com/Current Matters/Corporate Recovery Matters/Matilda Minerals Limited. aspx). Ferrier Hodgson. . Retrieved 2009-06-29.
[55] Tasker, Sarah-Jane (2008-10-22). "Matilda Minerals in administration as China sale fails" (http://www.theaustralian.news.com.au/ business/story/0,28124,24530966-36418,00.html). *The Australian*. . Retrieved 2009-06-29.

External links

- Tiwi Land Council (http://www.tiwilandcouncil.net.au/)
- Tiwi Islands Shire Council (http://www.tiwiislands.nt.gov.au/)
- Tiwi Creation Stories (http://www.aboriginalartonline.com/regions/tiwi2.php)
- Tiwi Islands travel guide from Wikitravel

Northern Territory Football League

Formerly	Northern Territory Football Association (NTFA) Northern Territory Football League (NTFL)
Sport	Australian rules football
Inaugural season	1916, Darwin, Northern Territory
No. of teams	8
Country(ies)	Australia
Most recent champion(s)	Wanderers
TV partner(s)	ABC1
Official website	ntfl.aflnt.com.au [1]

The **Northern Territory Football League** (NTFL) is an 8 team Australian rules football semi-professional league operating in Darwin in the Northern Territory.

The premier grade is the largest Australian rules football league in the Northern Territory. The league consists of a single division with under 14, under 16, under 18, reserves and open (professional) levels of competition.[2]

Most NTFL matches are played on Marrara Oval (TIO Stadium).

The NTFL regularly attracts high profile profile semi-professional players from interstate leagues due to its lack of salary cap and its season which allowing players to extend their playing season into their off-season.

Clubs

Current clubs

Club	Nickname	Home Ground	Entered competition	Premierships
St Marys	Saints	Marrara Oval	1952	28
Nightcliff	Tigers	Nightcliff Oval	1950	3
Darwin	Buffaloes	Tiwi Oval	1917	23
Wanderers	Eagles	TIO Stadium	1917	12
Waratah	Warriors	Gardens Oval	1917	14
Palmerston	Magpies	Southern Cross Oval	1971	3
Southern Districts	Crocs	Norbuilt Oval	1984	2
Wadeye	The Magic	Wadeye Oval	2011	0
Tiwi Bombers	Bombers	Marrara Oval	2007	0

Jumpers

History

See Australian rules football in the Northern Territory

The NTFL chose to play in the Northern Territory's 'wet season', primarily due to hard playing surfaces during the 'dry season'. Most other leagues in Australia operate during the winter, but since the Territory does not have a winter, it is played at different times.

The Wanderers Football Club were the founding members of the league in 1916. Waratah Football Club also joined in 1916 and are the only club to have competed in every single season since the formation of the league. Darwin (Buffaloe Football Club) was formed a year later in 1917. Nightcliff formed in 1950. St Marys formed in 1952. Palmerston entered the league in 1973 as North Darwin. Southern Districts entered the league in 1987. Tiwi Bombers entered 2006 with full entry in 2007

In the 1990s, the league ran into financial problems primarily due to the Northern Territory government luring the league to the new purpose-built stadium at Marrara Oval after its construction in 1991. The move pushed the league's operating costs up drastically despite contrary promises from the NT government. Marrara Oval is now known as TIO Stadium, as part of a naming rights deal with NT health insurance company Territory Insurance Office.

During this history of the league it has exported successful players to other leagues, notable players have included Michael McLean, Maurice Rioli and Michael Long.

Northern Territory Football League

In 2006, it was announced that a team representing the Tiwi Islands, called the *Super Tiwis* would be added to the 2006/07 season for eight games against teams that would normally have the bye. They will become a permanent part of the league in the 07/08 season as the Tiwi Bombers, clad in Essendon Football Club style guernseys of black and red.

There was also a push for an NTFL representative club to compete in the SANFL. The first of a series of trial matches was held in 2006, with a long term view of admitting a Darwin side into the SANFL. A strong crowd at Marrara Oval witnessed North Adelaide defeat a composite NTFL squad by 27 points, demonstrating that a Darwin team could be competitive. There is a push to make the event an annual match.[3]

The NTFL became an 8 team competition in the (07/08) with the full time inclusion of the Bombers.

However, the governing body of the NTFL decided on fielding a side in the AFL Queensland State League from 2009 and the Northern Territory Football Club was formed.

Audience

Attendance

The NTFL attracts strong local crowds. The 2005 Grand final attracted a crowd of over 5,000 people. One of the biggest crowds was the 2010/11 Grand Final between St Mary's and Wanderers, with the Muk Muks(wanderers) prevailing with a 28 point win, which attracted a over 9,000 strong crowd.

Media

Television

In 2006, NTFL matches were broadcast nationally for the first time ever on ABC2 each Sunday afternoon from February to March. Previously the matches had only been shown in the Territory on ABC Darwin. In 2008, it reverted to local broadcasting.

See also

- AFL Northern Territory

References

[1] http://ntfl.aflnt.com.au
[2] Official NTFL fixture (http://ntfl.aflnt.com.au/?s=results)
[3] NTFL vs North Adelaide (http://www.abc.net.au/nt/stories/s1564282.htm)

External links

- Official website (http://ntfl.aflnt.com.au)
- NTFL pages on Full Points Footy (http://www.fullpointsfooty.net/afl_northern_territory.htm)

AFL Northern Territory

AFL Northern Territory is the governing body for Australian rules football in the Northern Territory, Australia. It supervises multiple leagues, but is mainly concerned with the co-ordination of the Northern Territory Football League. The body is officiailly affiliated with the Australian Football League.

See also
- Australian rules football in the Northern Territory
- List of Australian rules football leagues in Australia

External links
- Official Site [1]

References
[1] http://www.aflnt.com.au

Marrara Stadium

Marrara Stadium

Former names	Marrara Stadium, Football Park
Location	Darwin, Northern Territory
Coordinates	12°23′57″S 130°53′14″E
Opened	1991
Owner	AFLNT
Operator	TIO Insurance and Banking
Surface	Grass
Capacity	15,000

Marrara Stadium (also known as *Football Park* and currently as **TIO Stadium** due to naming rights) is a sports ground in Darwin, Northern Territory, Australia. The ground was built in 1991 and Australian rules football and Cricket are primarily played at the venue. This includes Northern Territory Football League matches, pre-season Australian Football League matches, and also one AFL Premiership match each year - a 'home' game for the Western Bulldogs (although in 2009 there were two games). The record crowd of 17,500 was set in 2002 for an AFL pre-season practice match between the Aboriginal All-Stars and Carlton Football Club which the All-Stars won.

The stadium hosted two cricket Tests in 2003 with Australia against Bangladesh and 2004 against Sri Lanka, as well as a total of four one day internationals against Bangladesh in 2003 and 2008. The current total capacity is around 15,000 including 5,000 seats. In 2007 the Western Bulldogs played the Fremantle Dockers, in the Dockers' first home and away season game at the ground. Port Adelaide Power has also played five games at TIO against the Western Bulldogs, in 2004, 2006, 2008 and 2009. Port Adelaide also has had a three-year deal with the Northern Territory government and Marrara Stadium, that stats that Port would play two home and away games at TIO Stadium each year for three years starting in 2009.

TIO Stadium has hosted AC/DC for their "Ballbreaker" tour in November 1996, when 13,000 fans and 170 tonnes of equipment packed the ground. Sir Elton John performed for the first time in the Northern Territory, at TIO Stadium on the 17 May 2008 as part of the his Australian Tour.[1][2]

Marrara Stadium will play host to its first ever NRL match when the Sydney Roosters and North Queensland Cowboys clash in Round 7 of the 2012 NRL season[3]. It will also be the first NRL match played in the Top End in 21 years.

See also

- List of Test cricket grounds

References

[1] "Elton John to rock with the crocs" (http://www.abc.net.au/news/stories/2008/04/01/2205237.htm?section=entertainment). Australian Broadcasting Corporation. . Retrieved 2008-04-02.
[2] "Sir Elton rolls in for crocodile rock" (http://www.ntnews.com.au/article/2008/04/01/3760_ntnews.html). Northern Territory News. . Retrieved 2008-04-02.
[3] Darwin to host Cowboys and Roosters | News | NT News | Darwin, Northern Territory, Australia | ntnews.com.au (http://www.ntnews.com.au/article/2011/09/21/261801_ntnews.html)

External links

- Marrara Stadium (http://www.austadiums.com/stadiums/stadiums.php?id=69) at *Austadiums*

Traeger Park

Traeger Park is a small stadium located in Alice Springs, Northern Territory, Australia.

The stadium hosts Australian rules football and cricket matches and has a capacity of 10,000.

Traeger Park is home to the Central Australian Football League, and also hosts the annual Ngurratjuta Easter Lightning Carnival.[1]

Traeger Park has occasionally staged pre-season matches for the Australian Football League and National Rugby League. In 2004, an AFL Regional Challenge match between Collingwood Football Club and Port Adelaide Football Club attracted a sell-out crowd of 10,000. In 2006, the West Coast Eagles played the Carlton Football Club in an NAB Cup Regional Challenge match. A Trial match between the North Queensland Cowboys and the Brisbane Broncos was played at the ground during the warm-up to the 2011 NRL season.

Central Australian Football League match at Traeger Park, Alice Springs

References

[1] Edmund, Sam (30 April 2011). "Red heart's stronger pulse" (http://www.dailytelegraph.com.au/sport/afl/red-hearts-stronger-pulse/story-e6frexx0-1226047344419). . Retrieved 15 Dec 2011.

External links

- Traeger Park (http://www.austadiums.com/stadiums/stadiums.php?id=187) at *Austadiums*

Northern Territory Cricket

Northern Territory Cricket	
Logo of Northern Territory Cricket	
Formation	1978
Legal status	Incorporated association
Location	Fannie Bay, Darwin
Coordinates	12°25′26″S 130°50′10″E
Region served	Northern Territory
President	Bruce Walker
Affiliations	Cricket Australia
Website	ntcricket.com.au [1]

Northern Territory Cricket, formally the **Northern Territory Cricket Association**, is the governing body for cricket in the Northern Territory of Australia.[2] Cricket in the Northern Territory has produced state contracted players. Ken Skewes, Kane Richardson, Cameron Francis are all contracted to the South Australia Redbacks, whilst D'Arcy Short is playing for Western Australia.

Affiliations

The association is affiliated with Cricket Australia. The Alice Springs Cricket Association is a member association of Northern Territory Cricket.[3]

Competitions

The association is responsible for organising the Darwin and Districts cricket competition. The annual Imparja Cup Indigenous cricket tournament is hosted by Northern Territory Cricket.[4]

References

[1] http://www.ntcricket.com.au
[2] "Home Page" (http://www.ntcricket.com.au). Northern Territory Cricket. . Retrieved 2009-10-13.
[3] "Northern Territory Cricket Association Constitution" (http://www.ntcricket.com.au/docs/NTCA Constitution Dec '03.doc). Northern Territory Cricket. 2002. . Retrieved 2009-10-13.
[4] "Events - Imparja Cup" (http://www.ntcricket.com.au/imparjacup.php). Northern Territory Cricket. . Retrieved 2009-10-13.

Rugby league in the Northern Territory

Rugby league is administered by the Northern Territory Rugby League. Rugby league in the Darwin is played at Richardson Park, whilst Rugby league in Alice Springs is played at Anzac Oval.

History

The first organized competition played in Darwin. was in 1941 when 9 teams, mostly made up of ex-servicemen decided to make one unified competition and compete between and against each other. Some of the teams represented the Royal Australian Air Force, the Royal Australian Navy, and the Australian Army. There were also teams made up of citizens in Darwin, along with a team made up entirely of indigenous Australians living in Darwin.[1]

The competition was cancelled due to the bombing of Darwin and the air raid attacks on the city. Since most of the competition was made from ex-servicemen and the army divisions in Darwin, the competition was severely effected when many of these personal had to go to war and when they were no longer stationed in the Darwin area.

Another competition resumed in 1942 and continued onto 1943 (tt was a season which elapsed two years) but because of the evacuation of Darwin and then the subsequent shipping out of army and navy personnel from Darwin meant that the competition was completely halted. There appears to be no other competition formed between 1943 and 1949. After 1949, the competition was finally revived.

In 1950, a small group of men, mainly ex-servicemen, joined together to form the Northern Territory Rugby League. The first official season was started in 1950 in Darwin with a number of pre-season trial matches and tournaments. The first official match was played on 14 June 1951.

Cyclone Tracey smashed into Darwin on 24 December 1974 and completely devastated Darwin Although much damaged was done to its surroundings, fortunately however, little damage occurred on Richardson Park, the home of rugby league in Darwin. The cyclone had an effect on the competition itself as players and administrators of the clubs and boards of the competition either left Darwin or were involved in the clean-up in Darwin after the cyclone had subsided.

In recent years however, the league has expanded a little. It has picked in areas previously dominated by Aussie Rules Football. Some of the areas the league has moved into include the Katherine.

Governing body

The **Northern Territory Rugby League** is responsible for administering the game of rugby league in the Northern Territory of Australia. It controls the Darwin Rugby League, Darwin Junior Rugby League and the Centralia Australian Rugby Football League.

Northern Territory is an Affiliated State of the overall Australian governing body the Australian Rugby League.

Darwin Rugby League

Club	Suburb	Ground
Brothers (Darwin)	Anula	Anula Oval
Katherine Wests Tigers	Katherine	Sports & Recreation Club
Litchfield Bears	Litchfield	Freds Pass Reserve
Nightcliff Dragons	Nightcliff	Dripstone High School Oval
Palmerston Raiders	Palmerston	Archer Oval
South Darwin Rabbitohs	South Darwin	Mararra Sporting Complex
University Sharks	Casuarina	University Oval

Central Australian Rugby Football League

Club	Suburb	Ground
Wests Dragons	Alice Springs	ANZAC Oval
United Magpies	Alice Springs	ANZAC Oval
Vikings	Alice Springs	ANZAC Oval
Memo Bulls	Alice Springs	ANZAC Oval

Foundation teams are Wests Dragons and United Magpies.

Current Ground Announcer is Mick Gallagher

Katherine Rugby League

Club	Suburb	Ground
Katherine Bushrangers	Katherine	Sports & Recreation Club
Katherine Raiders	Katherine	Sports & Recreation Club
Katherine Wests Tigers	Katherine	Sports & Recreation Club

Gove Rugby League

Club	Suburb	Ground
Gove Rugby League	Gove / Nhulunbuy	

Popularity

Per capita figures show that the Northern Territory along with Queensland are the highest participators per capita of rugby league in Australia.

Representative Fixtures

The Northern Territory team play in the Affiliated States Championship along with the other three affiliated states (South Australia, Victoria and Western Australia) plus the Australian Police and Australian Defence Force. They won the title in 2004.

The Northern Territory competed in the Amco Cup in 1977, 1978 and 1987.

References

[1] *Sporting Pulse* Darwin Rugby League History Page (http://www.sportingpulse.com/assoc_page.cgi?c=7-719-0-52899-0&sID=3025) retrieved 21 December 2007

Further reading

- McPherson, A. Frank (2003). *The first fifty years: rugby league in the Northern Territory* (http://books.google.co.uk/books?id=Fw6aPAAACAAJ&source=gbs_navlinks_s). A.F. McPherson. ISBN 0646421468, 9780646421469.

External links

- The Northern Territory Rugby League (http://www.sportingpulse.com/assoc_page.cgi?c=1-2008-0-0-0&sID=17293)
- Rugby League clubs in the Northern Territory (http://www.playrugbyleague.com.au/nt/)

Northern Territory Rugby Union

The **Northern Territory Rugby Union** is responsible for rugby union in the Australian region of the Northern Territory, and is part of the Australian Rugby Union.

External links

- Official site [1]
- Rugby in NT [2]

References

[1] http://www.ntrugby.com.au/
[2] http://www.sportlinkup.nt.gov.au/find_a_sport/rugby_union

V8 Supercars

Category	Touring car racing
Country or region	Australasia
Inaugural season	1997
Drivers	28
Teams	17
Constructors	2
Tyre suppliers	Dunlop
Drivers' champion	Jamie Whincup
Teams' champion	Triple Eight Race Engineering[1]
Makes' champion	Holden[2]
Official website	V8Supercars.com.au [3]

Current season

V8 Supercars is a touring car racing category based in Australia and run as an International Series under Fédération Internationale de l'Automobile (FIA) regulations. As well as enjoying popularity in Australia, it has a considerable following in New Zealand, and is steadily growing in popularity across the world where television coverage allows.

V8 Supercar events take place in all the states of Australia, which is one of the only professional sports in Australia to boast such a feat. Overseas rounds are also held in New Zealand and Abu Dhabi and, up until 2010, Bahrain.[4] V8 Supercars have drawn crowds of over 250,000 spectators.[5] The 2010 season was held over 14 race weekends at purpose-built racetracks and street circuits. Race formats include sprint races, with either a 100 km or 200 km race on Saturday and one 200 km race on Sunday, two 250 km races over the weekend (Adelaide and Sydney), two 300 km races over the weekend (Gold Coast) or endurance races such as Bathurst, which runs over 1000 km race distance, and Phillip Island, which runs over 500 km.

The V8 Supercars themselves take as their basis either the Holden Commodore or Ford Falcon. Although they bear some resemblance to the production models outwardly, they are built from the ground up to suit the motorsport application. They are strictly governed in most aspects of performance in an effort to keep all the drivers on an even footing to create closer, more exciting racing. Because of this, entire fields of 28 drivers are at times separated by just one second over qualifying laps at some events.

The reason these two cars are used is their historical significance: Commodore and the Falcon are two of the most popular passenger-cars in the Australian car-market.

History

In January 1993 the Confederation of Australian Motor Sport replaced the existing Group 3A Touring Car category (formerly based on FIA Group A rules) with a new three-class Group 3A. This encompassed:

- Class A for Australian-produced 5.0 litre V8 engined Fords and Holdens
- Class B for 2.0 litre cars complying with FIA Class II Touring Car regulations
- Class C, valid for 1993 only, for normally aspirated two-wheel drive cars complying with 1992 CAMS Group 3A Touring Car regulations.[6]

Cars from all three classes would contest the Australian Touring Car Championship as well as non-championship Australian touring car events such as the Bathurst 1000; but for the purposes of race classification and points allocation, cars competed in two classes:

1. over 2000cc
2. up to 2000cc

Existing normally aspirated cars such as the BMW M3 could continue to compete under the Class C clause, unlike the turbocharged Ford Sierra and Nissan Skyline GT-R models which the new rules excluded from the category. However the M3 received few of the liberal concessions given to the new V8s and, with the Class C cars eligible for 1993 only, the German manufacturer's attention switched to the 2.0 litre class for 1994.

From 1995 the 2.0 litre cars, now contesting their own series as Super Touring Cars, became ineligible for the Australian Touring Car Championship. They did not contest the endurance races at Sandown and Bathurst, leaving these open solely to the 5.0 litre Ford and Holden models.

The category acquired the moniker 'V8 Supercars' in 1997 after event-management company IMG won the rights to the series in 1997 after a bitter battle against CAMS and the ARDC, and led the championship on a rapid expansion. Network Ten began televising the series in the same year, taking over from Channel Seven. The Australian Vee Eight Supercar Company (AVESCO) was later formed to run the series directly and later became an independent organisation from its IMG origins.

AVESCO introduced carnival street-race V8 Supercar events (such as the Clipsal 500) and strove to turn Australian touring car racing into a world-class product. The name "Shell Australian Touring Car Championship" was replaced by "Shell Championship Series", now called the "V8 Supercar Championship Series". In 2005 AVESCO changed its name to V8 Supercars Australia (VESA).[7][8]

In the Group 3A / V8 Supercar category, from 1993 to 2008, Holden drivers have won nine Australian Touring Car Championships/Shell Championship Series/V8 Supercar Championship Series titles and Ford drivers have won seven.

- List of Australian Touring Car and V8 Supercar Champions

The V8 Supercar

The regulations aim to balance the desire for technical competition and fast vehicles with a requirement to keep costs reasonable. Racing is close, and the cars bear some resemblance to production models. The application of "Project Blueprint" - introduced at the beginning of the 2003 season (where both makes of car were examined to ensure parity), has ensured that the racing between Holden and Ford has become closer than ever (reducing the risk of a series dominated by a single make).

The Ford Falcon of Craig Lowndes at Queensland Raceway, 2009

Bodyshell

Each V8 Supercar is based on a current-specification VE Commodore or FG Falcon production bodyshell, with an elaborate roll cage. In 2007, new rules stipulated both the Commodore and Falcon adopt composite front mudguards in place of the production steel items, in order to save costs. The composite guards are a homologated (fixed) laminate of fibreglass and aramid (or similar) fibres.

The Holden Commodore of Garth Tander at the L&H 500, 2008

The VE Commodore was initially rejected from taking part in the series due to its wheelbase being longer and wider than the BF Falcon. For the model to be homologated, V8 Supercar granted the Commodore a custom fabricated bodyshell into which a limited number of production bodyshell panels are incorporated. As a result, the roofline is lower than production and the rear door is shorter such that externally the rear doors, roof and rear quarters all consist of specialised custom coachwork panels.

Similarly, the longer wheelbase of the FG Falcon (over the BF) requires a comparable custom-fabricated shorter body, and the FG is also shortened in the rear door and lowered in the roof line compared to the road going model.

Aerodynamics

Cars have a standard "aerodynamic package" of spoilers and wings, a front splitter/air dam and side-skirts made in-house by the teams or bought from specialist companies. Testing was conducted by a representative team from each manufacturer so that in principle the two makes have similar aerodynamics. This is tested and measured by running both cars up to a set speed and then allowing to stop under friction, without the aid of brakes. This allows an accurate measure of aerodynamic drag over a broad range of speeds.

Weight

The minimum category weight is 1355 kg (2987 lbs.) (without the driver)

Power

A V8 Supercar must have a front-engine design and rear-wheel drive. Every car uses either a 5.0 L Ford "Boss 302" SVO or a 5.0 L Chevrolet small block race-engine (depending on the make) - capable of producing between 460 and 485 kW (620 — 650 bhp) of power, but generally quoted as a little over 450 kW (600 bhp) in race trim. Engines have pushrod actuated valves and electronic fuel injection. Both Ford and Holden engines are based on racing engines from their respective US parent companies. Engines are electronically restricted to 7,500 rpm.

Broadly speaking, the engines have a capacity of 5 litres, with 2 valves per cylinder. Compression ratio is regulated to 10:1. From the 2009 season onwards, cars run on E85 fuel consisting of 85% ethanol, which while reaping the benefits of a fuel largely made from a renewable resource has seen a marked increase in fuel consumption. EFI configuration is that of individual throttle bodies (albeit throttle actuation is linked/synchronised) and one injector per cylinder.

Engines typically produce approximately 50 less bhp when raced at the Bathurst 1000. This is done both to gain necessary engine longevity on the endurance race as well as to improve fuel efficiency, and moderate the number of potential refuelling stops. The advent of E85 fuel however has reduced the importance of fuel efficiency as a typical Bathurst stint has been reduced from approximately 31-32 laps to 22-23.

Some common components

All cars in the category use identical spool differentials, brake packages and gearboxes. The category uses a 6-speed Hollinger gearbox (Australian made), in either the 'H' pattern or as of 2008, a sequential pattern. Differential ratios used throughout the season are 3.75:1, 3.5:1, 3.25:1 and 3.15:1. The 3.15:1 ratio differential was introduced in 2005 to be used at Bathurst - cars with this ratio can now exceed 300 km/h (186 mph) on Conrod Straight (this has yet to be demonstrated, although Perkins Engineering claims to have exceeded this speed multiple times in the 2005 event). The theoretical maximum speed is 306 km/h (190 mph) at 7,500 rpm. All cars have a 75 litre fuel tank, except for the endurance races at Phillip Island and Bathurst (which still use the 120 litre fuel tank from previous seasons), the previous "Bathurst Tank" had a capacity of 120 litres.

Suspension

Basic front-suspension configuration is double wishbone (made compulsory for both makes through Project Blueprint), whilst rear suspension is a "live axle" design, using 4 longitudinal links and Watt's linkage for lateral location. Both suspension systems are similar to those fitted to the EL Falcon.

Brakes

Front- and rear-brake discs have to be made out of ferrous material (*steel brakes* as opposed to *carbon brakes*). Maximal dimensions for each disk are 376x35.56 mm (diameter x thickness). Until the end of the 2006 season, teams could choose the manufacturer of the braking system. In 2007 the UK-based brake-manufacturer Alcon secured a contract to supply the braking system in accordance with specific regulations.

Tyres

A Dunlop "control tyre" is supplied to all teams. Throughout the year, there are restrictions on the number of testing days (6 per year), along with the number of tyres used during those days. For race meetings, teams are allocated a set number of tyres for the entire weekend, with the number available for each race depending on the type of race (sprint or endurance).

The series adopted a softer, higher performance "sprint tyre" during the 2009 season — although it was not used during every race meeting. The idea is to allow every driver to use one set of those softer tyres, that can be used at the team's own discretion. A source of controversy is that the soft tyre set is allocated per weekend, meaning each driver has to choose which race they wish to maximise their performance, with the other race potentially sacrificed. It has added an element of contrivance to race results with front running competitors languishing downfield through no fault of their own, and allowing midfield drivers to win races.

Cost

Reported to be approximately A$600,000 per car and A$130,000 per engine. Teams spend up to A$10 million per year running their two-car teams. TEGA introduced a salary cap of A$6.75 million in order to keep costs down in 2007, called the Total Racing Expenditure Cap (TREC). It was scrapped after only one season.

Future

In the middle of 2008, a working group known as the "Car of the Future" project and led by former driver Mark Skaife was organised by V8 Supercars to investigate future directions for the sport. The working group had the primary objective of cutting costs to just A$250,000 per car, with a projected timeline of introducing the new formula for the 2012 season. The plan was unveiled in March 2010 at Crown Casino and incorporated several key changes to the internal workings of the car, with the differential, brakes, cooling and fuel systems all changed to a control - or identical - component for all cars, as well as changes to the rear suspension and engine.[9] Notably, the Car of the Future plan aims to encourage more manufacturers to enter the sport - provided that they have four-door saloon cars currently in mass production.[10] While the plans were well-received by all of the teams, Holden chief Simon McNamara warned potential new manufacturers to stay out of the championship just hours after the plans were released, claiming that they would "gain nothing" from entering the series,[11] (which as of 2010 fields twice as many Holdens as Fords).

Along with the release of the Car of the Future plans, V8 Supercars Australia Chairman Tony Cochrane detailed plans dubbed "Phase Two", intended to look at the direction of the sport in the first five years of the Car of the Future's introduction. In addition to more manufacturers, Phase Two plans include adding to the sport's international appeal by including races in India, Korea, Hong Kong, Singapore and South Africa, as well as two brand-new domestic races.[12] [13]

In addition to the Phase Two plans, the FIA has announced that V8 Supercars will head to the Circuit of the Americas in Austin, Texas in 2013.[14]

In August 2011, it was revealed that V8 Supercars Australia was in the process of negotiating to hold a race at Clark International Speedway in the Philippines from 2013.[15]

Championships

Three separate V8 Supercar series exist. The primary series is the "Level One" championship called the 'International V8 Supercars Championship'. A "Level Two" championship, referred generically as the V8 Supercar Development Series, and presently know by the commercial identity as the Fujitsu V8 Supercar Series, was originally intended for privateers who formerly raced in the Level One series but have been left behind by increasing pace of the professional teams, however, some "Level One" teams run secondary teams in the Fujitsu series to "blood" new drivers or as a secondary income stream for drivers without a team of their own. The only way to compete in the "main game" is to purchase a licence from an existing team (TEGA are no longer involved in creating new licences for V8 teams).

A third series for older V8 Supercars, the V8 Touring Car National Series, was held for the first time in 2008. Presently known as the Kumho V8 Touring Car Series this series runs on the programme of the Shannons Nationals Motor Racing Championships, V8 Supercar Australia have no involvement in the running of this series and race cars have to be de-registerred from involvement in the Fujitsu Series prior to being run in this series.

Race formats

Each round in the series follows either a sprint- or endurance-race format. All rounds include practice, qualifying, and racing in some form.

Warm up

A warm-up session of about 20 minutes takes place before the endurance races.

Practice

Practice sessions normally happen over a single two-hour session for sprint races; over two half-hour sessions - or four sessions of varying lengths - for enduros.

Qualifying

Qualifying includes two legs. Leg 1 takes 20 minutes, with all drivers competing (30). Leg 2 is 15 minutes long and includes 20 of the drivers from the previous session. The top 10 drivers then compete in a "Top Ten Shootout", where each driver gets one lap to set the fastest possible time.

L&H 500 features two qualifying sessions of 20 minutes for each driver in the entry. After the time trials there go two 14-lap races, each for an entry driver with championship points awarded at conclusion. Sum of the points for the entry determines start position at the main event. This system is a little similar to Daytona 500 qualifying procedure.

V8 Supercar first adopted the leg-based qualifying system in 2001, although have not used it consistently. 2008 saw a return to this method, utilising a system much the same as Formula One. 2009 saw the return of a NASCAR style top ten shootout for the top ten grid positions.

In 2009 a controversial rule change determined the drivers' starting position for the entire race meeting from their qualifying position. This was changed before the Hamilton 400 to a system with separate qualifying sessions for each race. It remains in use currently.

In 2010, they now hold three qualifiers, where in the first 20 minute stint those who fall outside the top 10 start on the grid as they finish. The second qualifier those outside the top 10 start the race as they finished the qualifier and the those in the top 10 battle it out for pole position. However, in the endurances top 10 shootouts are still there.

Endurance races

The L&H 500 involves a single race run over a distance of 500 km (310 mi). Compulsory pitstops are taken for tyres, driver changes and fuel. It is held at Victoria's Phillip Island Grand Prix Circuit.

The Bathurst 1000 comprises a single race run over a distance of 1000 km (620 mi) (161 laps of the Mount Panorama circuit), with the same rules for pitstops plus brake pad changes also. The teams are given 24 tyres per car for the weekend.

2010 will see the beginning of the Gold Coast 600 which comprises two 300 km races over a weekend. Each car will have two drivers, with up to 17 international drivers in total invited to participate in the event.

Clipsal 500

The Clipsal 500 consists of two races run over a distance of 250 km (160 mi) (78 laps) each with compulsory pitstops for both fuel and tyres. The teams are given 16 tyres for the weekend.

Sprint races

From 2009, for all other rounds, two races over 200 km (120 mi) each take place across the weekend. Pit-stops are not compulsory, as they have been in the past, however every team must put in a minimum of 50 litres per race. The longer race format and E-85 fuel blend compared to previous years mean the cars must refuel to be able to complete race distance. From rounds 2-7 of 2006, the second race of the sprint round was made a reverse grid race, in an effort to spice up the action. Unfortunately, this initiative was unpopular with fans, drivers, and team owners, because it was expensive (repairing cars that otherwise wouldn't have been damaged), and didn't really make the racing any better. Teams are given 12 tyres per car for the weekend.

Marquee events

The Bathurst 1000, Clipsal 500, Sydney Telstra 500 and L&H 500 are the marquee events of the V8 Supercar calendar. In 2005 there was also a marquee round in Shanghai, however the promoter discontinued with this race in 2006.

Bathurst 1000

Known as the "Great Race", the Bathurst 1000 is a traditional 1000 km test of drivers, teams and machines held at the Mount Panorama Circuit in Bathurst, New South Wales. It has been the pre-eminent domestic motor racing event in Australia for decades - well before the development of the V8 Supercar category. It is conducted over 161 laps, on a track that features two long straights, that contrast with a tight section of fast blind corners across the top of the mountain.

2008 Safety Car

In the early years, the race was open to almost anybody with a car that met (considerably more relaxed) regulations and held an Australian motorsport licence. The resulting wide variety of cars, driver talent, and budgets ensured that large margins split the placings. In the modern V8 era, the field has consisted of professional teams only.

The introduction of the safety car, which brings the field together when an accident makes the track unsafe, has radically changed the nature of the race. But Bathurst has always been an intensely tactical race, hinging on pit stop strategy (fuel economy, tyres, etc.) driver talent and outright overall speed.

The 2006 Bathurst 1000 became a very emotional event to all drivers, teams, friends and fans of one of its greatest drivers in its history, 9 time winner of the "Great Race", Peter Brock (killed in the Targa West rally event the month before). The inaugural and perpetual Peter Brock Trophy was handed out to eventual race winner Craig Lowndes and Jamie Whincup. An emotional Lowndes, who was a protégé of Peter Brock, dedicated his win to his mentor.

V8 Supercars Australia has banned fulltime drivers from racing together at the endurance races, including Bathurst, from 2010 onwards.[16]

Clipsal 500

The Clipsal 500 is held in Adelaide on a shortened version of the former Grand Prix Circuit. The event in the heart of the city has a carnival atmosphere, and crowds of over 200,000 racing fans and socialites turn out each year. Two 250 km races are held on each of Saturday and Sunday, and this has proven to be a very successful format. It is the first event to be inducted into the V8 Supercar Hall of Fame and is a winner of various awards. While the trophy presentation is centred around the results of race two, the round winner is decided by points accrued from both races. In 2009 the two races were formally separated.

Jamie Whincup celebrating winning the 2008 Clipsal 500

Phillip Island 500

The 500-kilometre (310 mi) Phillip Island 500K endurance race is held at the Phillip Island Grand Prix Circuit in Victoria. The race is sponsored by Lawrence & Hanson and is known as the L&H 500.[17]

The race takes over from the Sandown 500 after the Sandown round was downgraded to a sprint round in 2008 because of the condition of the facility.[18] [19]

Grand Finale

AVESCO created a special season ending round. Initially this round was held as the thirteenth championship event in late November at Eastern Creek Raceway near Sydney. It was sponsored by VIP Petfoods and was branded 'The Main Event'. The round was won by Marcos Ambrose in a fitting conclusion to his 2003 championship win, but made headlines when Ambrose's teammate Russell Ingall and Holden Racing Team rival Mark Skaife spectacularly brought the sport into disrepute with an on-track/off-track stoush. In 2004 the event became known as the 'Bigpond Grand Finale', and was again held at Eastern Creek - won again by Marcos Ambrose. In 2005 the venue moved to the Phillip Island Grand Prix Circuit as the final round of the championship and the base for Russell Ingall's series win. In 2006, the event was known as the 'Caterpillar Grand Finale'. Todd Kelly won in controversial circumstances, with two race wins (race one and two) and a fifth placing (race three). His brother, Rick Kelly, won the championship after he was given a drive through penalty for a collision with title contender, Craig Lowndes. The collision caused Lowndes major steering damage that required Kelly only to finish the race to win the championship. However the championship was not decided until the day after in a court appeal in Melbourne in which Lowndes' Triple 8 Engineering team lost.

2008 saw the event moved to Oran Park Raceway as a dual finale for both the 2008 series, as the veteran Sydney circuit's closure was imminent. For 2009 the new Sydney Telstra 500 event held the Grand Finale, with James Courtney winning the race.

Hall of Fame

The V8 Supercar Hall of Fame, instituted in 1999, adds new recipients each year at the end-of-year prizegiving ceremony held just after the final round in December. Recipients have mostly not been V8 Supercar drivers but from the Australian Touring Car Championship era and have been multiple winners of the ATCC or the Bathurst 1000. In a controversial exception, in 2005 the Adelaide 500 race was inducted.

Organisation

V8 Supercars Australia manages, markets, and promotes the V8 Supercars sport. It is a joint venture between Touring Car Entrants Group of Australia (TEGA - 75%) and Sports & Entertainment Limited (SEL - 25%).[20] It is run by an eight-member board. Four representing TEGA, two representing SEL, and two independent directors.[21][22]

It was founded in 1997 under the name the Australian Vee Eight Supercar Company (AVESCO). TEGA was responsible for the rules and technical management of the series and the supply of cars and drivers while SEL was responsible for capturing and maintaining broadcasting rights, sponsorship, licensing and sanction agreements.[20] In 2005 it changed its name to V8 Supercars Australia to make it more identifiable with the sport.[7][8] In 2008 the separate boards of V8 Supercars Australia and TEGA were combined into a single board that is solely responsible for administering the sport.[21][22]

Television coverage

From the 2007 season onwards Seven Network has broadcast the V8 Supercars. Channel Seven secured the rights and took over from Network Ten, which had successfully broadcast the events since taking over from Seven in 1997. The deal is worth roughly A$120 million. Channel Seven will show increased live coverage, as well as a weekly 25-minute show specific to the series on non-racing weekends. The coverage however is produced by V8 Supercar Television, a specialist production vehicle for V8 Supercars Australia.

As of 2010 Network Ten continues to broadcast V8 Supercar once a year when they appear on the support program for the Australian Grand Prix, a Network Ten broadcast event. All support category races are tied up with the Grand Prix broadcast rights as a package. The Albert Park Race is a non-championship event.

Television One provided coverage of all rounds in New Zealand until the end of the 2007 season, at which time coverage transferred to TV3.

- Australia
  - Seven Network
  - Speed Channel (subscription television)
  - Telstra Bigpond Broadband (Live Internet Coverage)
- International
  - TV3 (New Zealand)
  - Motors TV (United Kingdom, Republic of Ireland, France, Germany, the Netherlands and most other parts of Europe)
  - Neo Sports + India
  - Speed Channel (USA, Canada, Caribbean and Latin America): coverage is hosted by current NASCAR driver and former V8 Supercar champion Marcos Ambrose on a week delay except Surfers Paradise and Bathurst starting in 2011. Beginning in 2011, Bathurst and Surfers Paradise are broadcast live as Saturday evening US Eastern Time broadcasts in 720p (HDTV). 2011 Bathurst and Gold Coast rounds had a commentary team of Leigh Diffey, Mike Joy, Darrell Waltrip, and Calvin Fish on site.

- Australia Network - Asia-Pacific region (except New Zealand) and parts of the Middle East. (NB: Except for the Bathurst 1000, All Races will be screened on delay on the Australia Network.)

V8 Supercars Television records the series in 16:9 (576i), with many cars carrying 4 or more mini cameras. High-definition was used to broadcast the 2011 Bathurst 1000 and the Gold Coast 600, it was the first time that V8 Supercars races were available in HD.[23] For North American audiences, the 2011 Bathurst 1000 and Gold Coast 600 races that aired on Speed live with a full Charlotte-based production crew on site were screened in 16:9 720p high definition coverage, as the network's live motorsport coverage is usually screened in high-definition format.[24]

Records

Driver championships			Driver round wins			Driver starts			Team round wins			Manufacturer round wins		
Pos.	Driver	Titles	Pos.	Driver	Wins	Pos.	Driver	Starts	Pos.	Team	Wins	Pos.	Manufacturer	Wins
1	Ian Geoghegan	5	1	Mark Skaife	42	1	John Bowe	225	1	Holden Racing Team	67	1	Holden	205
2	Dick Johnson	5	2	Craig Lowndes	38	2	Mark Skaife	220	2	Dick Johnson Racing	45	2	Ford	166
3	Mark Skaife	5	3	Peter Brock	37	3	Peter Brock	212	3	Triple Eight Race Engineering	44	3	Nissan	25
4	Bob Jane	4	4	Allan Moffat	32	4	Glenn Seton	208	4	Holden Dealer/Advantage Racing	34	4	BMW	15
	Allan Moffat	4	5	Jamie Whincup	28	5	Russell Ingall	204		Allan Moffat Racing	34	5	Chevrolet	10
	Jim Richards	4	6	Dick Johnson	22	6	Dick Johnson	202	6	Gibson Motor Sport	32	6	Mazda	8
7	Peter Brock	3		Jim Richards	22	7	Craig Lowndes	193	7	Stone Brothers Racing	22	7	Volvo	5
	Craig Lowndes	3	8	Garth Tander	19	8	Tony Longhurst	191	8	HSV Dealer Team	19	8	Jaguar	4
	Jamie Whincup	3	9	Glenn Seton	17	9	Steven Richards	188	9	Glenn Seton Racing	17	9	Porsche	2
10	3 drivers tied with two championships each						2 drivers tied with 15 races each	10		10 184	Perkins Motorsport			

Note: bold text indicates active drivers, teams and manufacturers.

Note: The above records relate to the Australian Touring Car Championship (1960-1998), the Shell Championship Series (1999-2001), the V8 Supercar Championship Series (2002-2010) and the International V8 Supercar Championship Series (2011)

* While 2009-2011 regulations do not recognise event winners, V8 Supercar does officially track event winners for statistics purposes.[25]

* Figures accurate to 2011 Telstra Sydney 500.

See also

- Australian Touring Car Championship
- List of Australian Touring Car and V8 Supercar champions
- List of Australian Touring Car Championship races
- Australian Production Car Championship
- V8 Supercars RedLine, an immersive racing simulator at Dreamworld

References

[1] 2010 V8 Supercar Championship Series Team Points (http://www.v8supercar.com.au/tabid/86/entity/team/season/6/series/1/default.aspx) Retrieved on 22 December 2010
[2] "V8 Supercars champion James Courtney claims award double" (http://www.perthnow.com.au/sport/motor-sport/supercar-champion-james-courtney-claims-v8-award-double/story-e6frg26l-1225966593782). .
[3] http://www.v8supercar.com.au
[4] Musolino, Adrian (2010-10-29). "2011 Calendar" (http://www.v8supercars.com.au/newsarticle/2011-calendar-released/tabid/70/newsid/10615/default.aspx). Official site of the Australian V8 Supercar Championship Series. . Retrieved 2010 11 07.
[5] South Australia - Clipsal 500 Adelaide (http://www.southaustralia.com/9002347.aspx)
[6] CAMS Manual of Motor Sport, 1993, page 205
[7] V8 Supercars Australia: Name change to reflect continued growth (http://www.pando.com.au/sponsorshipnews/releases/release/27354.html)
[8] Name change for V8 body (http://www.foxsports.com.au/story/0,8659,17254127-23770,00.html)
[9] Gunther, Briar (2010-03-29). "Car of the Future released" (http://www.v8supercars.com.au/car-of-the-future-released/tabid/70/newsid/9848/default.aspx). *V8Supercars.com.au* (BigPond Sport). . Retrieved 2010-03-30.
[10] Musolino, Adrian (2010-03-29). "CoF opens the showroom floor" (http://www.v8supercars.com.au/cof-opens-the-shopfront/tabid/70/newsid/9849/default.aspx). *V8Supercars.com.au* (BigPond Sport). . Retrieved 2010-03-30.
[11] Phelps, James (2010-03-29). "Holden warn off Nissan and Toyota in V8 Supercars powerplay" (http://www.dailytelegraph.com.au/sport/motor/holden-warn-off-nissan-and-toyota-in-v8-supercars-powerplay/story-e6frey5r-1225847111813). *DailyTelegraph.com.au* (The Daily Telegraph). . Retrieved 2010-03-30.
[12] Gunther, Briar (2010-03-29). "Phase two engaged" (http://www.v8supercars.com.au/phase-two-engaged/tabid/70/newsid/9850/default.aspx). *V8Supercars.com.au* (BigPond Sport). . Retrieved 2010-03-30.
[13] Edwards, Alan (2010-03-29). "V8's future plans" (http://www.v8supercars.com.au/v8's-future-plans/tabid/70/newsid/9741/default.aspx). *V8Supercars.com.au* (BigPond Sport). . Retrieved 2010-03-30.
[14] Paukert, Chris (2011-06-30). "Official: V8 Supercar Series coming to Austin in 2013" (http://www.autoblog.com/2011/06/30/v8-supercar-series-coming-to-austin-in-2013). *autoblog.com* (AOL Autos). . Retrieved 2011-06-30.
[15] http://www.speedcafe.com/2011/08/17/v8-supercars-linked-to-race-in-philippines/
[16] Musolino, Adrian (13 December 2009). "Bathurst change is to the detriment of the great race" (http://www.theroar.com.au/2009/12/13/bathurst-change-is-to-the-detriment-of-the-great-race/). *The Roar*. . Retrieved 2009-12-13.
[17] L&H 500 at Phillip Island gets major makeover for big race (http://www.v8x.com.au/cms/A_110090/article.html)
[18] Phillip Island 500 here to stay (http://www.foxsports.com.au/story/0,8659,23262653-23770,00.html)
[19] Phillip Island 500 set to stay (http://www.drive.com.au/Editorial/ArticleDetail.aspx?ArticleID=49137)
[20] A success story - V8 Supercars Australia (http://www.v8supercar.com.au/content/about_avesco/the_v8_supercars_australia_success_story/)
[21] Streamlined board points V8 Supercars to big future (http://www.nzmotorsport.co.nz/content/newsarticle.cfm?id=13880)
[22] V8SC: V8 Supercars board streamlined (http://www.touringcartimes.com/news.php?id=2085)
[23] "Bathurst 1000 live in HD" (http://www.tvtonight.com.au/2011/09/bathurst-1000-live-in-hd.html). 2011-09-20. .
[24] V8: Bathurst 1000 and Gold Coast 600 live on Speed (http://auto-racing.speedtv.com/article/v8-bathurst-1000-gold-coast-600-live-on-speed/)
[25] v8supercars.com (http://www.v8supercars.com.au/Results/MostATCCV8SCRoundEventWinners/tabid/854/Default.aspx)

External links

Series

- The Official V8 Supercars Australia site (http://www.v8supercar.com.au)
- Clipsal 500 official site (http://www.clipsal500.com.au)

Teams

- Holden Racing Team (http://www.hrt.com.au/racing/2011/home)
- Stone Brothers Racing (http://www.stonebrothersracing.com.au/)
- Tony D'Alberto Racing (http://www.wilsonsecurityracing.com.au/index.php?filter=v8)
- Ford Performance Racing (http://www.fpr.com.au/)
- Rod Nash Racing (http://www.rodnashracing.com.au/)
- Kelly Racing (http://www.kellyracing.com.au/)
- Brad Jones Racing (http://www.bradjonesracing.com.au)
- Britek Motorsport (http://www.fairdinkumshedsracing.com.au/)
- Triple F Racing (http://www.triplefracing.com.au/)
- Dick Johnson Racing (http://www.djr.com.au/)
- Tekno Autosports (http://www.jonathonwebb.com/)
- Walkinshaw Racing (http://www.bundabergracing.com.au/bundy/2011/gateway/?RefPage=/bundy/2011/home/default.aspx)
- Lucas Dumbrell Motorsport (http://www.ldmotorsport.com.au)
- Garry Rogers Motorsport (http://www.grmotorsport.com.au/html/s01_home/home.asp)
- Paul Morris Motorsport (http://www.paulmorris.com.au)
- Team Vodafone (Triple Eight Race Engineering) (http://www.teamvodafone.com.au)

Skycity Triple Crown

Venue	Hidden Valley Raceway
Race Format	
Race 1	
- Laps	34
- Distance	100 km
Race 2	
- Laps	69
- Distance	200 km
Last Race (2010)	
Winning Driver	Jamie Whincup
Winning Team	Triple Eight Race Engineering
Winning Manufacturer	Holden

I+ style="font-size:larger;" |Skycity Triple Crown

The **Skycity Triple Crown** is a V8 Supercar event held annually at Hidden Valley Raceway near Darwin in the Northern Territory, Australia.

Australia's northernmost racetrack had existed for several years prior to its upgrade for its national championship debut in 1998.

The event is staged over a three-day weekend (Friday-Sunday). Practice is held on Friday. During most of its history the meeting was held to a three race format with the first race held on Saturday and two on Sunday. 2009 saw the adoption of the two stand alone races format with individual qualifying each day for each race.

Past winners

- 1998 Russell Ingall
- 1999 Jason Bright
- 2000 Mark Skaife
- 2001 Marcos Ambrose
- 2002 Mark Skaife
- 2003 Marcos Ambrose
- 2004 Todd Kelly
- 2005 Todd Kelly
- 2006 Craig Lowndes
- 2007 Craig Lowndes
- 2008 Steven Richards
- 2009 R1 Jamie Whincup
- 2009 R2 Michael Caruso

Darwin Football Stadium

Darwin Football Stadium	
Full name	Darwin Football Stadium
Location	Marrara, Northern Territory
Coordinates	12°23′47″S 130°52′51″E
Built	2007
Opened	28 July 2007
Owner	Northern Territory Government
Surface	Grass
Construction cost	A$6.5m
Capacity	6000

Darwin Football Stadium is a sports stadium in Darwin, Australia in the Marrara Sporting Complex.

Work began on the stadium in 2007 and was officially opened on 28 July 2007 when it played host to an A-League Pre-Season Cup game between Perth Glory and Melbourne Victory.

The stadium has a seating capacity for up to 1,120 spectators, but can hold up to 6,000 including standing space.

External links

- Darwin Football Stadium [1] - at Austadiums

References

[1] http://www.austadiums.com/stadiums/stadiums.php?id=301

Football Federation Northern Territory

The **Football Federation Northern Territory** is the state governing body for association football (soccer) in the Northern Territory, Australia. It is affiliated with Football Federation Australia, the national governing body. The Territory is also separated into three (Northern, Central and Southern) zones which have their own zone councils which administer leagues locally running their own league and cup competitions.

There is currently no overall champion - the regional winners in 2006 were Darwin Olympic (Northern Zone) and Verdi (Southern Zone). There was no competition in the Central Zone.

Clubs in NT

Northern Zone

2009 Premier League Teams

- Casuarina Football Club
- Darwin Olympic Soccer Club
- Hellenic Athletic Club
- Darwin Dragons Soccer Club formerly Marrara Dragons Soccer Club
- Nakara Azzuri Football Club
- Padres Football Club
- Palmerston Football Club
- Port Darwin Football Club

Past Participant Clubs

- Darwin City Buffalos
- Darwin Lions (Pre-2007 known as Afro-Oz Football Club)
- Karama United Football Club
- Litchfield Soccer Club
- Mindil Aces Soccer Club
- University Rangers Football Club
- Waratahs Soccer Club (2007 No longer a Registered Club)

Central Zone

- Borroloola FC
- Gove Soccer Club
- Katherine FC

Southern Zone

- ASFA - (Not registered club, Academy team)
- Buckleys Football Club (Pre-2007 known as Town and Country Tavern)
- Celtic Soccer Club (2007 No longer a Registered Club)
- Federals Soccer Club
- Scorpions Soccer Club
- Stormbirds Football Club
- Verdi Soccer Club
- Vikings Football Club

External links

- Football Federation Northern Territory Official website [1]

References

[1] http://www.footballnt.com.au/

North Queensland Fury F.C.

Full name	North Queensland Fury Football Club
Nickname(s)	The Fury
Founded	2008
Dissolved	2011
Ground	Dairy Farmers Stadium Townsville Queensland Australia (Capacity: 26,500)
Owner	Football Federation Australia
Chairman	Rabieh Krayem
Coach	František Straka
League	A-League
2010–11	11th
Home colours Away colours	

North Queensland Fury FC were a professional football (soccer) club based in Townsville, Queensland, Australia, which competed in the A-League. North Queensland played its home fixtures at Dairy Farmers Stadium. The club was closed on 1 March 2011, due to financial instability.

History

A Townsville bid was first considered for the 2007–08 season, when the New Zealand Knights' licence was revoked. A group named *Tropical Football Australia* attempted to secure the spot but Football Federation Australia preferred to keep a New Zealand team in the competition, opting for the Wellington Phoenix.[1]

A bid known as *Northern Thunder FC* (or *North Queensland Thunder FC*) was considered for admission for the 2008–09 season along with Gold Coast Galaxy. The bid was publicly well progressed, with the teams badge and colours (red, white and black) released. The training facilities were to be located at the North Queensland Institute of Sport and the home ground was to play at Dairy Farmers Stadium.

The bid was tentatively accepted to join in the 2008–09 season expanding the league to ten teams. Needing to meet certain financial criteria to be granted entry into the league, the club's major financial backer pulled out of the franchise on 5 March 2008, effectively collapsing the bid. Football Federation Australia determined on 11 March 2008 that neither Thunder or Galaxy would be granted entry "in the best interests of the league," given that a nine team format was generally unfavoured and delayed expansion of the league until the 2009–10 season.[2] [3]

With expansion put off until the following season, by June 2008 the FFA had received ten bids for new A–League teams, two of which came from Townsville – one headed by Melbourne businesswoman Milissa Fischer and one by local businessman Don Matheson.[4][5] Matheson's bid, which "rose from the ashes of the Northern Thunder bid",[6] was granted a provisional licence by Football Federation Australia on 24 July.[7][8] On 27 August 2008 the franchise was accepted into the A–League by CEO Ben Buckley with the only matter outstanding the finalisation of all legal requirements.[9]

On 6 November 2008, the franchise named was officially revealed as North Queensland Fury FC.[10] Their inaugural kit was revealed in April 2009, featuring dark green sleeves/socks, and a white/light green front.[11]

It was announced on 10 December 2008, that the Fury had signed Rockhampton–born businessman Dean Hassall as their CEO.[12] Also the club signed Scottish club, Celtic's strength and conditioning coach Alan McCall.[13]

North Queensland in the 2009/2010 season won the 'Queensland Nickel Cup', which was a tri-tournament played throughout the regular A League season between the Queensland clubs of North Queensland, Brisbane Roar and Gold Coast United.

Season two

At the end of the 2009–10 season the club was reportedly under severe financial pressure following lower than expected crowds. The Fury were expecting a crowd average of over 8,000 as opposed to an actual average of 6,723. Losses were estimated as high as $50,000 per week, with an expected first year loss of $4 to $5 million. Don Matheson handed back the franchise license as he was unable to continue to pay these large losses on his own. Organisationally the existing club company was shut down, and all existing contracts at the club were cancelled.

Inaugural coach Ian Ferguson left the club and accepted the assistant manager role at fellow A-League club Perth Glory. Some players from their inaugural season were re-signed on new terms. These were David Williams, Dyron Daal, Justin Pasfield, Jack Hingert, Ufuk Talay and Osama Malik. The rest of the squad was assembled prior to a new coach being put in place and largely comprised young players and some who were released from other A-League clubs. The FFA chose to have the club operate at the minimum 85% of the salary cap, as some other clubs in the competition also choose to do of their own accord. This was done to reduce the cost of the playing staff wages. All players were signed on to a 1 year deal with the exception of David Williams who had been re-signed on a 2 year deal.

On 7 June 2010, former Sparta Prague and one time Czech Republic national team coach František Straka was announced as the clubs coach for the coming 2010–11 A-League season after agreeing to a one-year deal.[14]

North Queensland Fury started the 2010/2011 with many of their new players performing above expectations despite their match record being poor. They were generally outclassed, but played with an energy, passion and commitment that caught the imagination of fans across the league. New manager Franz Straka proved to be a charismatic figurehead for the club's new dawn.

With the exception of David Williams, as per A-League regulations, all the players having signed only 1-year deals become free agents in October 2010. They, along with all other players on 1-year contracts or on the final year of multi-year contracts, are allowed to be approached by other teams for followings season. In this case, the 2011/2012 season. FFA decided not to re-sign any of their current players or attempt to sign new ones for the following season, as the future of the club beyond the current season was not assured.

The club finished last in the 2010/11 A-League season, winning only 4 of their 30 matches. The crowd average of 4,245 was the 4th lowest in the history of the A-League behind the Gold Coast United crowd average of the same season and the two seasons of the New Zealand Knights.

Demise

A community ownership model was launched, aimed at finding 1.5 million dollars (per year, for three years), of capital investment being sought to cover half the expected losses for the next three seasons. Ben Buckley, in an open letter to Fury supporters, made it clear that the FFA could not fund continual losses.[15]

On 1 March 2011, the club officially had its A-League license revoked due to financial reasons. The FFA reported that the Fury had received only $300,000 of the investment required for the next season, and despite increased sponsorship revenue the club would still lose $2 to $3 million dollars. FFA released a statement confirming earlier reports that a decision had been taken not to continue with the franchise as the financial position of the club for season 2011-2012 considered too big of a financial risk for the FFA to undertake.[16]

Colours and badge

North Queensland's colours were light and dark green and white. These were chosen to represent the lush green vegetation of the northern parts of Queensland. The badge was revealed in 2008 soon after the bid was granted entry to A–League. The light green was often referred to in the local media as "tropical green" but was particularly unpopular with many fans of the club.

Stadium

The club's home ground was the Willows Sports Complex, although it is currently known as Dairy Farmers Stadium due to sponsorship rights. It is situated in Townsville, Queensland, Australia. The stadium's capacity is 26,500

Supporters

After it was announced that Townsville's bid for a team was successful, fans set out to establish a supporters group in conjunction with the Fury board. After much debate the name *F-Troop* was settled on. The name was intended to encompass both the military history of the town and the club name. F-Troop gained a boisterous and impressive reputation for loud active support on match days.

Rivalries

Given the location of the club in North Queensland, there were no clubs that could be classed as a local rival. However, given the status of Gold Coast United as the other new team to the A-League and both clubs' status as Queensland clubs a rivalry was developed between the two. This was intensified by the Fury's 5–0 thrashing at the hands of Gold Coast in their second A-League game, whilst Fury gained a measure of revenge in the following away game, beating the Gold Coast two-nil, with a double from Robbie Fowler. On 13 February 2010, in the final game of the regular season, NQFC again defeated the Gold Coast, 2–1, at Dairy Farmers Stadium, in front of their 2nd highest home crowd of the season: 8517. Many Fury fans use the abbreviation "FTB" whenever they referred to Gold Coast United or their fans online.

Brisbane Roar was also considered rivals due to their being a Queensland club as well (and North Queensland Fury's closest geographical opponent), the first competitive match between the clubs ended 1–1, Fowler scoring for the Fury. Fans of North Queensland Fury believed that the 1354 kilometres between Townsville and Brisbane makes fixtures between North Queensland Fury and Brisbane Roar the largest geographical "local derby" in world football.

Affiliated clubs

- Capricorn Cougars
- Far North Queensland Bulls
- North Queensland Razorbacks
- Whitsunday Miners

All-time A-League Win/Loss (including finals)

Last updated 19 February 2011

Club	Pld	W	D	L	GF	GA	GD
Adelaide United	6	1	1	4	8	19	-11
Brisbane Roar	6	0	3	3	4	9	-5
Central Coast Mariners	6	0	2	4	5	12	-7
Gold Coast United	6	3	0	3	7	13	-6
Melbourne Heart	3	0	0	3	2	6	-4
Melbourne Victory	6	1	2	3	3	8	-5
Newcastle Jets	6	1	0	5	5	12	-7
Perth Glory	6	3	3	0	10	7	3
Sydney FC	6	3	1	2	8	9	-1
Wellington Phoenix	6	0	3	3	5	11	-6
Total	57	12	15	30	57	106	-49

International Teams Wins/Loss

Club	Pld	W	D	L	GF	GA	GD
Hekari United	1	1	0	0	4	1	3
Tampines Rovers	1	0	0	1	0	1	-1
Wolverhampton Wanderers	1	0	0	1	1	2	-1
Total	3	1	0	2	5	4	1

Players who earned International caps whilst at North Queensland

- Shane Stefanutto
- David Williams
- Jeremy Brockie
- Eugene Sseppuya

Notable former players

See also List of North Queensland Fury FC players

Australia

- Rostyn Griffiths
- Osama Malik

North Queensland Fury F.C.

- 🇦🇺 Robbie Middleby
- 🇦🇺 Shane Stefanutto
- 🇦🇺 Isaka Cernak
- 🇦🇺 Gareth Edds
- 🇦🇺 Simon Storey
- 🇦🇺 David Williams
- 🇦🇺 Justin Pasfield
- 🇦🇺 Chris Grossman
- 🇦🇺 Chris Payne
- 🇦🇺 Daniel McBreen
- 🇦🇺 Jason Spagnuolo
- 🇦🇺 Paul Henderson
- 🇦🇺 Chris Tadrosse
- 🇦🇺 Matt Smith
- 🇦🇺 Ufuk Talay

Germany
- 🇩🇪 Andre Kilian

England
- 🏴󠁧󠁢󠁥󠁮󠁧󠁿 Robbie Fowler
- 🏴󠁧󠁢󠁥󠁮󠁧󠁿 Mark Hughes

New Zealand
- 🇳🇿 Jeremy Brockie

Togo
- 🇹🇬 Eric Akoto

Uganda
- 🇺🇬 Eugene Sseppuya

Honours

- 🇦🇺🇺🇬 **Queensland Nickel Cup**
    - 2009/10 (NQ Fury V's Gold Coast United: {Contested Over 3 League Fixtures} NQ Fury W2/D0/L1)
- 🇦🇺🇺🇬 **Chief Minister's Cup**
    - 2009 (3-2 V's Adelaide United - Played In Darwin/NT 02/07/09)

All Time League Records

- **Record Victory:** 2-0 vs Gold Coast United (A), 31 October 2009
- **Record Defeat:** 1-8 vs Adelaide United (A), 21 January 2011
- **Highest League Crowd:** 8,897 vs Sydney FC, 8 August 2009
- **Lowest League Crowd:** 2,866 vs Melbourne Heart, 10 November 2010
- **Winning Streak:** 2 games (24 October 2009 – 31 October 2009)
- **Undefeated Streak:** 5 games (3 October 2009 – 31 October 2009)
- **Losing Streak:** 8 games (2 January 2011 - Continuing)
- **Winless Streak:** 11 games (18 December 2010 - Continuing)
- **Goals in a game:** 2 - Robbie Fowler vs Gold Coast United (A), 31 October 2009 and Dyron Daal vs Newcastle Jets (A), 20 December 2009

- **Goals in a season:** 9 - Robbie Fowler, 2009/10
- **Most Assists in a season:** 4 - Robbie Fowler, 2009/10 & Chris Payne 2010/11
- **Most Appearances:** 49 - David Williams

See also

- 2009-10 North Queensland Fury FC season
- 2010–11 North Queensland Fury FC season
- List of North Queensland Fury FC players

References

[1] "Kiwis alive as Townsville pulls pin" (http://www.foxsports.com.au/story/0,8659,21407148-5000940,00.html). Fox Sports. 2007–03–19. . Retrieved 2007–03–19.
[2] "No A–League Expansion This Season" (http://au.fourfourtwo.com/news/71821,no-aleague-expansion-this-season.aspx). FourFourTwo. 2008–03–11. . Retrieved 2008–05–27.
[3] "Hyundai A–League expansion delayed" (http://www.a-league.com.au/default.aspx?s=hal_newsdisplay&id=21732). A–League. 2008–03–11. . Retrieved 2008–03–11.
[4] "Interest aplenty for new A–League clubs" (http://news.theage.com.au/sport/interest-aplenty-for-new-aleague-clubs-20080603-2l97.html). The Age. 2008–06–03. . Retrieved 2008–08–18.
[5] "FFA to consider 10 new bids for expanded A–League" (http://www.abc.net.au/news/stories/2008/06/03/2264178.htm). ABC News. 2008–06–03. . Retrieved 2008–08–16.
[6] "North Qld FC confident of success" (http://theworldgame.sbs.com.au/a-league/north-qld-fc-confident-of-success-120089/). The World Game. 2008–06–04. . Retrieved 2008–08–18.
[7] "North Queensland FC awarded exclusive negotiating status" (http://www.footballaustralia.com.au/InsideFFA/default.aspx?s=insideffa_newsfeatures_newsitem&id=22912). Football Federation Australia. 2008–07–24. . Retrieved 2008–08–16.
[8] "Townsville given provisional A–League licence" (http://www.townsvillebulletin.com.au/article/2008/07/25/14906_sportsphoto.html). Townsville Bulletin. 2008–07–25. . Retrieved 2008–08–18.
[9] "Expansion Gets Go Ahead" (http://www.a-league.com.au/default.aspx?s=newsdisplay&id=23378). A-league.com. 2008–08–28. . Retrieved 2008–09–16.
[10] "North Queensland Fury at Launch" (http://au.fourfourtwo.com/news/88425,north-queenland-fury-at-launch.aspx). au.fourfourtwo.com. 2008–11–06. . Retrieved 2008–11–06.
[11] http://mattwintersfootballblog.blogspot.com/2009/04/north-queensland-fury-kit-revealed.html
[12] "Fury announces new CEO" (http://www.northqueenslandfc.com.au/default.aspx?s=newsdisplay&id=25415). www.northqueenslandfc.com.au. 2008–12–10. . Retrieved 2008–12–10.
[13] "Townsville A–League team turns up heat with extra coach" (http://www.townsvillebulletin.com.au/article/2009/01/08/31845_sportsphoto.html). Townsville Bulletin. 2009–01–8. . Retrieved 2009–01–08.
[14] http://au.fourfourtwo.com/news/168040,furys-czech-mate.aspx
[15] , "Clearing air over the Fury" (http://www.townsvillebulletin.com.au/article/2010/12/16/193021_fury.html)
[16] , "Fury Kicked Out Of The A-League" (http://www.foxsports.com.au/football/a-league/north-queensland-fury-dropped-from-a-league-after-being-unable-to-front-15million-for-licence/story-e6frf4gl-1226014174045?from=public_rss), Fox Sports

External links

- North Queensland Fury FC Official Website (http://www.northqueenslandfc.com.au/)
- Official photographs of the North Queensland Fury FC 2010 Awards night (http://www.cameronlaird.com/nqfury2010awards/)

Sport in Australia

Australia has a sporting history dating back to the mid 1800s. By the 1920s, a number of sports were being played by both men and women, including cricket, badminton, judo, swimming, tennis, netball, lacrosse, golf, hockey and various codes of football.

Many Australians participate in sport, including association football (soccer), athletics, Australian rules football, baseball, basketball, cricket, cycling, golf, gymnastics, horse racing, motor racing, netball, rugby league, rugby union, shooting, swimming, tennis and tenpin bowling. Australia's climate lends itself to some sports, such as swimming, more than others, such as snowboarding.

There are a number of professional sport leagues in Australia, including the A-League, ANZ Championship, the Australian Football League (AFL), the National Basketball League, National Rugby League (NRL), Super Rugby, the W-League and the Women's National Basketball League. Attendance for some of these leagues over the course of a single season tops one million spectators in

Bondi Icebergs Club at dawn

leagues like the AFL and NRL. The media plays an important part in Australia's sporting landscape. Many sporting events are televised or are covered by the radio. The government has anti-siphoning laws to protect free-to-air stations. Beyond televising live events, there are many sport television shows, sport talk shows on the radio, magazines dedicated to sport, and extensive newspaper coverage. Australian sport has also been the subject of Australian made films such as *The Club* and *The Final Winter*.

As a nation, Australia has competed in many international events including the Olympics and Paralympics, the Commonwealth Games and sport specific events like the FIFA World Cup and the Cricket World Cup. The country has a large number of national teams in sports such as association football (soccer), basketball, hockey, netball, rugby league, rugby union, softball, water polo and wheelchair rugby. Women's sport first really began in Australia in the 1880s. Netball is one of the most popular women's sports in the country. Competitive disabled sport exists in Australia, with the country having a national women's deaf association football (soccer) team, and competing in major events such as the Summer and Winter Paralympics.

History

1800s

The first Australian cricket team which played overseas was the 1868 Aboriginal cricket tour of England. The Australian team which toured England in 1948 was nicknamed The Invincibles and was captained by Donald Bradman. In recent years the Australia team has been captained by Allan Border, Mark Taylor, Steve Waugh, Ricky Ponting, and currently Michael Clarke.[1]

As early as the 1820s, there are reports of Rugby games being played at Barrack Square in the city between the army and the crews of visiting ships. Rugby Union formally began in Australia with the formation of the first clubs, the oldest of which is the Sydney University Club, formed in 1864.By 1874 there were enough clubs to form a Sydney Metropolitan competition and

Cricket players, ca. 1881.

in that year the Southern Rugby Union was established. In 1892 the Southern Rugby Union of New South Wales and the Northern Rugby Union of Queensland (formed in 1883) became New South Wales and Queensland Rugby Unions respectively.[2]

Representatives from these two unions combined in 1899 when an Australian team played its first Test series - against a visiting team from the British Isles. Four tests were played, Australia winning the first test at the Sydney Cricket Ground 13-3. The second test in Brisbane and the third and fourth Sydney were won by the British Isles who took out the series. Without a national jersey, the Test matches in New South Wales were played in blue jerseys and in Queensland in maroon - both with the Australian Coat of Arms on their chests. In 1903 Australia and New Zealand played a single test at the Sydney Cricket Ground in front of a crowd of 30,000. This was the beginning of intense rugby rivalry between the two nations. The crowd had grown to almost 50,000 at the same venue when Australia played New Zealand in 1907.[2]

Rugby was the most popular sport in both New South Wales and Queensland. In 1907 there were movements within Rugby about creating a breakaway competition and playing under the Northern Union (laser renamed 'Rugby League') Rules. In 1908 the first Australian Rugby League competition started, which is now the NRL. Over the next few years the new sport Rugby League took over as the dominate sport in New South Wales and Queensland.[3]

The VFA is formed in Melbourne in 1877.[4]

Australia's first lawn tennis court was built on Garden Island on Sydney Harbour in 1880. It is still in use.[5] [6] [7]

The first recorded association football (soccer) game took place in Hobart on 10 May 1879 when the Cricketers Football Club played a scratch match. The first recorded inter-club match took place a month later when the Cricketers took on New Town FC on 7 June.[8] The oldest existing club is Balgownie Rangers, founded in 1883, which still competes in the Illawarra regional league.[9]

Athletics Australia (AA) was created in 1897, with men's and women's associations amalgamating in 1978.[10]

The family of "Swimming Professor" Richmond Theophillus "Dick" Cavill (1884–1938) contributed significantly to the development of the sport of swimming: his son Arthur is credited by some with originating the Australian crawl stroke, which now predominates in "freestyle" swimming races. Another son, Sydney, was the originator of the butterfly stroke. Youngest son Richmond Theophilus was the first to use the crawl in a competition, winning 100 yards State championship in 1899 and in England, in 1902, he was the first to swim 100 yards in under a minute.[11]

Eight clubs break away from the VFA to form the VFL in 1896.[12]

1900s

The Adelaide Oval, second day of the third test between Australia and England, 20 January 1902.

Start of the first McDonnell & East foot race from East Brisbane to Tingalpa, 1909 Scene on the corner of Wellington Road and Stanley Street East, with the Australian National Hotel on the left behind the racers.

The first Badminton competition in Australia was played in 1900.[13]

Judo was first demonstrated in Australia in 1906.[14]

The Australian Rugby League (ARL) was founded in 1907 as the governing body for the sport of rugby league in Australia.[15]

The first Australia-wide association football (soccer) body was the Commonwealth Football Association, formed in 1912, although this folded two years later.

1920s

Following World War I, in 1921, the Australian Soccer Association was formed which superceeded the defunct Commonwealth Football Association which folded in 1914. The first international association football (soccer) match Australia competed in was a friendly match against New Zealand in Dunedin on 17 June 1922.

In 1922, a committee in Australia investigated the benefits of physical education for girls. They came up with several recommendations regarding what sports were and were not appropriate for girls to play based on the level of fitness required. It was determined that for some individual girls that for medical reasons, the girls should probably not be allowed to participate in tennis, netball, lacrosse, golf, hockey, and cricket. Football was completely medically inappropriate for girls to play. It was medically appropriate for all girls to be able to participate in, so long as they were not done in an overly competitive manner, swimming, rowing, cycling and horseback riding.[16]

Group of tennis players, ca. 1922.

Dick Eve won Australia's first Olympic diving gold medal in 1924.[17]

1940s

Australian women's sports had an advantage over many other women's sport organisations around the world in the period after World War II. Women's sport organisations had largely remained intact and were holding competitions during the war period. This structure survived in the post war period. Women's sport were not hurt because of food rationing, petrol rationing, population disbursement, and other issues facing post-war Europe.[18]

Canoeing and Kayaking Australia was founded in 1947[19] with Australians winning 15 Olympic medals.[20]

1950s to present

In 1960 the Australian Soccer Association was suspended from FIFA for the poaching of players from overseas. In 1961 the Australian Soccer Federation (ASF) was formed. The federation is now known as Football Federation Australia. Australia's first national association football (soccer) competition, the National Soccer League was founded in 1977, this was superceeded by the A-League in 2005.

Participation

There are 34,000 athletes, officials and coaches currently registered with the Athletics Australia.[21] A 2007 estimate claimed that Australian football had 615,549 participants,[22] Basketball has become one of the most popular participation sports in Australia. In Victoria, and Melbourne, particularly, it has more participants than any other sport.[23] [24] [25]

Association football (soccer) is the only code of football that appears in the Australian top ten sports and physical recreational Activities by participation.[26]

Beach cricket being played at Cottesloe Beach in Perth.

Australia's warm climate and long coastline of sandy beaches and rolling waves provide ideal conditions for water sports such as swimming. The majority of Australians live in cities or towns on or near the coast, and so beaches are a place that millions of Australians visit regularly.[27]

Australia receives year-round snow in the Australian Alps and parts of Tasmania, and has indoor ice rinks in many cities. As a result, Australians are able to participate in a wide variety of winter sports, including skiing, snowboarding, cross-country skiing, biathlon, freestyle skiing (including aerial skiing and moguls), ice hockey, curling, short track speed skating and figure skating. Australia has Olympic programs for some of these sports. Australia has little or no facilities for ski jumping, and the ski runs are mostly too short for the faster competitive alpine skiing events like Super-G and Downhill. There are no bobsleigh tracks (used for bobsleigh, luge and skeleton) within Australia (the nearest one is in Japan), although Australia competes in slide events overseas, and there is a bobsleigh push track in the Docklands in Melbourne.[28]

Sport	Total Participation	Year	Participation % [29]	Year	Ref
Association football (soccer)			7.7%	1998/1999	[30]
Athletics	34,000	2006			[21]
Australian rules	615,549	2007	20.1%	1998/1999	[22] []
Baseball	57,000	2003			[31]
Basketball	1,000,000	2010	10.2%	1998/1999	[] [32]
Cricket			11.7%	1998/1999	[]
Cycling			3.4%	1998/1999	[30]
Golf			9.9%	1998/1999	[]
Gymnastics	120,000	2011			[33]
Horse racing			3.9%	1998/1999	[]
Motor car racing			3.5%	1998/1999	[]

Netball		3.8%	1998/1999	[]
Rugby league		10.7%	1998/1999	[]
Rugby union		5.4%	1998/1999	[]
Shooting	120,000	2007		[34]
Swimming		18.0%	1998/1999	[]
Tennis		3.9%	1998/1999	[]
Tenpin bowling		3.8%	1998/1999	[]

Professional sport

There are several professional and semi-professional sport leagues in Australia. They include the A-League, ANZ Championship, the Australian Football League, the National Basketball League, National Rugby League, the National Wheelchair Basketball League, Super Rugby, the Women's National Basketball League, and the Women's National Wheelchair Basketball League. Beyond that, there is professional horse racing and motor sport.

The National Basketball League was formed in 1978 and is Australia's top professional basketball competition. In its most recently completed season in 2010–11, it had eight teams in the country, plus one team in New Zealand.[32]

A match at Etihad Stadium, one of Melbourne's two major AFL venues.

Throughout its history, horse racing has become part of the Australian culture and has developed a rich and colourful language. The most famous racehorses of Australia's turf include the New Zealand bred Carbine, Phar Lap, and Tulloch, the Australian bred Bernborough, Gloaming and Kingston Town plus the British bred Makybe Diva.[35] Harness racing is another code of horse racing in Australia. Standardbred horses either trot, in a diagonal gait, or more usually pace (in a lateral gait), along with 8-12 other horses and drivers on a circular racing track over 600 to 1,400 metres. One of the most successful pacers in Australia was the New Zealand bred, Cardigan Bay who won 82 races in all and was the first Standardbred horse to earn (US) one million dollars or more.[36]

Melbourne Tigers and Gold Coast Blaze at State Netball and Hockey Centre

Spectatorship

In the 2006/2007 season, Melbourne Victory averaged 27,728 people to their home matches throughout the season. The 2009-10 regular season was considerably lower.[37] In 2008, the Australian Football League had a cumulative attendance of 7,083,015, a record for the competition and an average attendance of 38,295.[38] In 2010, the National Rugby League's premiership set a record for regular season attendance to NRL matches.[39]

Australian Open tennis

Leagues/Tournaments	Total spectatorship	Year	Average match attendance	Year	Ref
A-League			8,752	2010/2011	[40]
Australian Football League	7,139,272	2011	36,425	2011	[41]
Horse racing	2,000,000	2002/2003			[42]
National Basketball League	547,021	2010/2011	4,031	2010/2011	[32]
National Rugby League	3,465,851	2011	17,243	2011	[43]
Rugby League State of Origin	186,607	2011	62,202	2011	[44]
Women's National Basketball League	77,944	2010/2011			[32]

Amateur sport

Amateur sport is often organised top down by national federations. These organisations include Athletics Australia and Swimming Australia.

Sport media

Media coverage of Australian sport and athletes predates 1876. The first all Australian sport publication, *The Referee*, was first published in 1886 in Sydney.[45] The major newspapers for sport coverage in the country include *The Courier Mail* and *The West Australian*.[]

the 1967 NSWRFL season's grand final became the first football grand final of any code to be televised live in Australia. The Nine Network had paid $5,000 for the broadcasting rights.[46]

SBS and FoxSports are two of the most important television networks in Australia in terms of covering all Australian sports, not just the popular professional leagues.[] Administrators for less popular spectator sports, such as basketball and netball, believe that getting additional television and newspaper coverage is fundamental for the growth and success of their sports going forward.[]

Sky Sports Radio

Anti-siphoning laws in Australia regulate the media companies' access to significant sporting events. In 1992, when the country experienced growth in paid-subscription media, the Parliament of Australia enacted the Broadcasting Services Act that gave free-to-air broadcasters preferential access to acquire broadcasting rights to sporting events.

The **anti-siphoning list** is a list of major sporting events that the Parliament of Australia has decided must be available for all Australians to see free of charge and cannot be "siphoned off" to pay TV where people are forced to pay to see them. The current anti-siphoning list came into effect in 2006 and expires 31 December 2010. The Minister for Communications can add or remove events from the list at his discretion. There are currently ten sports on the anti-siphoning list plus the Olympic and Commonwealth Games. Events on the anti-siphoning list are delisted 12 weeks before they start to ensure pay TV broadcasters have reasonable access to listed events, if free-to-air broadcasters decide not to purchase the broadcast rights for a particular event. Any rights to listed sporting events that are not acquired by free-to-air broadcasters are available to pay TV. For multi-round events where it is simply not possible for free-to-air networks to broadcast all matches within the event (e.g. the Australian Open) complementary coverage is available on pay television. The Federal Government is obliged by legislation to conduct a review of the list before the end of 2009. The current anti-siphoning list requires showing listed sports on the broadcaster's main channel.[47]

Sport is widely televised in Australia. The table below contains ratings information for 2011 matches and television shows for the National Rugby League and the Australian Football League and other sporting events.

2011 OzTem Five Television Ratings

Match	Network	Air date	OzTam Five city Live	Sydney	Melbourne	Brisbane	Adelaide	Perth	Ref
2011 Supercheap Auto Bathurst 1000	Channel 7	9-Oct-11	1212000	384000	302000	287000	153000	86000	[48]
2011 NRL Grand Final	Nine	2-Oct-2011	2027000	1021000	347000	524000	48000	87000	[49]
2011 NRL Grand Final Presentation	Nine	2-Oct-11	1548000	893000	***	511000	60000	84000	[]
2011 AFL Grand Final	Ten	1-Oct-11	2595000	258000	1367000	308000	297000	365000	[50]
2011 AFL Grand Final Post Match Presentation	Ten	1-Oct-11	2106000	187000	1114000	257000	276000	271000	[]
2011 AFL Grand Final Pre Game	Ten	1-Oct-11	1932000	141000	1096000	229000	204000	262000	[]
2011 AFL Grand Final Pre Match Entertainment	Ten	1-Oct-11	1405000	800000	863000	151000	147000	164000	[]
The Footy Show (rugby league) season final	Nine	29-Sept-11	973000	152000	507000	116000	128000	71000	[51]
2011 Singapore Grand Prix	OneHD	25-Sept-11	280000	55000	84000	50000	40000	52000	[52]
2011 Brownlow Medal	Channel 7	26-Sept-11	1130000	16000	743000	6000	156000	210000	[53]
Rugby League Final Series Pf2	Nine	24-Sept-11	1174000	619000	274000	274000	4000	2000	[54]
Ten's AFL Finals 2011: 2nd Prelim. Final Geelong V West Coast	Ten	24-Sept-11	1095000	57000	556000	79000	118000	284000	[]

The table below gives an idea as to the viewing audience.

League	Aggregate audience	Year	Total television viewers	Year	Average per game	Year	Ref
National Basketball League			6,061,679	2010/2011	33,815	2010/2011	[32]
National Rugby League	128,500,000	2009					[55]
Women's National Basketball League			1,352,096	2010/2011			[32]

Rugby league had the highest aggregate television ratings of any sport in 2009[56] and 2010.[57] Also, in a world first, the Nine Network broadcasted free-to-air the first match of the 2010 State of Origin series live in 3D in New South Wales, Queensland and Victoria (not in SA or WA).[58][59]

There are a number of Australian sport films. They include *The Club*. The film was based on a play produced in 1977, in Melbourne. It has been in the senior English syllabi for four Australian states for many years.[60] The film was written by David Williamson, directed by Bruce Beresford and starring John Howard, Jack Thompson, Graham Kennedy and Frank Wilson.[61] Another Australian sport film is *The Final Winter*, released in 2007. It was directed by Brian Andrews and Jane Forrest and produced by Anthony Coffee, and Michelle Russell, while independently produced it is being distributed by Paramount Pictures. It was written by Matthew Nable who also starred as the lead role 'Grub' Henderson. The film, which earned praise from critics,[62] focuses around Grub who is the captain of the Newtown Jets football team in the early 1980s and his determination to stand for what rugby league traditionally stood for while dealing with his own identity crisis.[63]

Sport is popular on the radio. This Sporting Life was a culturally iconic Triple J radio comedy programme, created by award-winning actor-writer-comedians John Doyle and Greig Pickhaver, who performed as their characters Roy and HG. Broadcast from 1986 to 2008, it was one of the longest-running, most popular and most successful radio comedy programmes of the post-television era in Australia. IT was the longest-running show in Triple J's programming history, and commanded a large and dedicated nationwide audience throughout its 22-year run.[64] 2KY is a commercial radio station based in Sydney, broadcasting throughout New South Wales and Canberra on a network of over 140 narrowcast transmitters as well as the main 1017 AM frequency in Sydney. 2KY broadcasts live commentary of thoroughbred, harness and greyhound racing. Over 1500 races are covered each week, including the pre and post race form and TAB betting information.[65]

There are a number of Australian sport magazines. One is the AFL Record. The magazine is published in a sports magazine style format. Eight different versions, one for each game, are published for each weekly round, 60,000 copies in total, and Roy Morgan Research estimates that the *Record* has a weekly readership of over 200,000.[66] As of 2009, the week's records are published and are able to be viewed in an online magazine format.[67] Another Australian sporting magazine is Australia's Surfing Life, a monthly magazine about surfing published in Australia. It features articles about surf trips in Australia and overseas, surfing technique, board design and wetsuits. The magazine was founded in 1985.[68]

International competitions

Each year, Athletics Australia conducts the Australian Championships and the Athletics Grand Prix Series, which are the main avenues for Australian athletes to qualify for the Olympic Games, Commonwealth Games and World Championships.[69]

Australian track cyclists Jack Bobridge, Anna Meares and Shane Kelly.

Each year Australia competes in various Rugby League and Rugby Union international competitions. Rugby League events include the Four Nations and the Rugby League World Cup. Rugby Union events include The Rugby Championship and the Rugby Union World Cup.

Till 2011, Australia has won the Cricket World Cup four out of the ten times it has been held. Australia dominated world cricket from the mid-90s to the end of the 2000s, but with retirement of many leading players they have dropped to 5th in the test rankings below India, South Africa, England and Sri Lanka. They have appeared in every world cup final from 1996 to 2007, and has been undefeated in world cup matches where they have gone on to win every single world cup match they have since played except for tying South Africa in the 1999 semi-final. This winning streak which spanned 4 World Cups and 34 games came to an end in March 2011 when they were defeated by Pakistan at the R. Premadasa Stadium in Colombo by 4 wickets.[1]

Australia has generally been a world power in Olympic swimming since the 1956 Melbourne Olympics: swimmers like Dawn Fraser, Kieren Perkins and Ian Thorpe have taken multiple gold medals.[70]

The Australian accocaition football (soccer) team appeared at the FIFA World Cup for the first time in 2006 and again in 2010. In their debut world cup appearance at the 2006 FIFA World Cup, the Socceroos surprised many by reaching the Round of 16, losing 1-0 in injury time to the eventual champions Italy.[71] Australia are four time winners and two otime runner-up of the OFC Nations Cup before moving to the Asian Football Confederation in 2006. Australia first appeared in the AFC Asian Cup in 2007 and were runners up in 2011. Australia will host the 2015 AFC Asian Cup.

Seven has exclusive Australian free-to-air, pay television, online and mobile telephony broadcast rights to the 2008 Summer Olympics in Beijing. The live telecast of the XXIX Olympiad was shared by both the Seven Network and SBS Television. Seven broadcast the opening and closing ceremonies and mainstream sport's including swimming, athletics, rowing, cycling and gymnastics. In stark contrast, SBS TV provided complementary coverage focused on long-form events such as football, road cycling, volleyball, and table tennis.[72]

National teams

Sport	Team (link to team / event)	Nickname (link for origin)	Name sponsor
Rugby union	Men's test	*Wallabies*.[73]	Qantas[73]
	Women's	*Wallaroos*[74]	Paper to Paper[75]
Rugby league	Men's test	*Kangaroos*[76] [77]	VB [78]
	Women's	*Jillaroos*[79] [80]	
	Wheelchair rugby	Paralympic	*Steelers* (official[81]) *Wheelabies* (unofficial[82] [83])
Association football (soccer)[84]	Men's	*Socceroos*	Qantas
	Women's (incl. Olympic)	*Matildas* (from *Waltzing Matilda*)	Westfield

Futsal[85]	National team	*Futsalroos*	Qantas
Gridiron (American football)	National team	*Australian Outback* — formerly *Australian Cyclones* (1999),[86] *Australian Bushrangers* (1997)[87]	
Netball[88]	National team	*Diamonds*	
Swimming[89]	Olympic, Paralympic, and World Championships	*Dolphins*	Telstra
Softball	Men's	*Aussie Steelers*[90]	
	Women's (Olympic / World's)	*Aussie Spirit*[91]	
Water polo	Men's	*Sharks*[92]	
	Women's	*Stingers*	
Basketball[93]	Men's	*Boomers*	Golden Star
	Women's	*Opals*	Jayco
	Intellectual disability (men)	*Boomerangs*	
	Intellectual disability (women)	*Pearls*	
Wheelchair basketball[93]	Men's	*Rollers*	
	Women's	*Gliders*	
Cycling	World Championships/World Cup	*Cyclones*[94]	Toshiba
Field hockey	Men's[95] [96]	*Kookaburras*	
	Women's[95] [96]	*Hockeyroos*	None for 2007 (ANZ for 2004 Olympics)[97]
Ice hockey	Men's	*Mighty Roos*[98] (after *The Mighty Ducks*)	
Lacrosse	Men's	*Sharks*	
Box lacrosse	Men's	*Boxaroos*[99]	
Bowls	Men's	*Jackaroos* — a pun on *jack*, the target ball[100]	
	Women's	*Sapphires*[101]	
Orienteering	National team	*Boomerangs*[102]	
Handball	Men's	*Crocodiles*[103]	
	Women's	*Redbacks*[103] [104]	
Ultimate Frisbee[105]	Open	*Dingos*	
	Women's	*Firetails*	
	Mixed	*Barramundis*	

Women's sport

While not being urged to avoid competition, women had few opportunities to compete in sport in Australia until the 1880s. After that date, new sporting facilities were being built around the country and many new sport clubs were created.[106]

Australia v England: International netball test – Adelaide, October 2008.

Netball is the most popular women's team participation sport in Australia.[107] In 1985, there were 347,000 players.[108] In 1995, there were over 360,000 Australian netball players.[109] Throughout most of Australia's netball history, the game has largely been a participation sport; it has not managed to become a large spectator sport.[109] In 2005 and 2006, 56,100 Australians attended one to two netball matches. Of these, 41,600 were women.[30] 46,200 attended three to five netball matches, with 34,400 of those spectators being women.[30] 86,400 attended six or more netball matches, with 54,800 spectators being female.[30] Overall, 188,800 people attended netball matches, with 130,800 being female.[30] In 2005 and 2006, netball was the 10th most popular spectator sport for women with Australian rules football (1,011,300), horse racing (912,200), rugby league (542,600), motor sports (462,100), rugby union (232,400), association football (soccer) (212,200), harness racing (190,500), cricket (183,200) and tennis (163,500) all being more popular.[30] The country set an attendance record for a netball match with a record crowd of 14,339 at the Australia–New Zealand Netball Test held at the Sydney SuperDome game in 2004.[110]

In 1940, a study of 314 women in New Zealand and Australia was done. Most of the women in the study were middle class, conservative, Protestant and white. The study found that 183 participated in sport. The ninth most popular sport that these women participated in was billiards, with 3 having played the sport. The sport was tied with croquet, billiards, chess, fishing, field hockey, horse racing, squash, table tennis and shooting.[18]

Disabled sport

The Deaf Matildas are the Australian women's national deaf association football (soccer) team.[18] Their first major tournament was the Deaflympic Games held in Australia in 2005.[18]

Australia sent a delegation to compete at the *2008 Summer Paralympics* in Beijing. The country sent 121 officials[111] and 170 athletes in 13 sports to Beijing. It was the country's largest ever Paralympic delegation.[112] The delegation's chef de mission was Darren Peters.[111] Australia sent 11 competitors to compete in two disciplines at the *2010 Winter Paralympics* in Vancouver, Canada.[113] The delegation also consisted of 3 sighted guides and 17 support staff. This was the largest delegation Australia had sent to a Winter Paralympics.[114]

Australian swimmers at the training pool at the 1996 Atlanta Paralympic Games

Notes

[1] "Cricinfo" (http://www.espncricinfo.com/icc_cricket_worldcup2011/engine/match/433596.html). *Match Scorecard.* .
[2] "rugby.com.au | History of the ARU" (http://www.aru.rugby.com.au/aru_hq/history_of_the_aru/history_of_the_aru,183.html). Aru.rugby.com.au. 1949-11-25. . Retrieved 2011-11-24.
[3] "A Brief History of Rugby League" (http://library.thinkquest.org/3369/rugby/past.htm). Library.thinkquest.org. . Retrieved 2011-11-24.
[4] "Victorian Football Association - Entry - eMelbourne - The Encyclopedia of Melbourne Online" (http://www.emelbourne.net.au/biogs/EM01557b.htm). eMelbourne. 2010-02-25. . Retrieved 2011-10-30.
[5] Elbourne, Sean (Winter 2006). "Wonderful Kuttabul - a long history of service" (http://www.navy.gov.au/w/images/Sea_Talk_2006-autumn.pdf) (PDF). *Sea Talk (Winter 2006)* (Royal Australian Navy): pp. 11–19. . Retrieved 2008-09-07.
[6] "Island's tourism birth a date with history" (http://www.smh.com.au/articles/2002/11/21/1037697802931.html). *The Sydney Morning Herald.* .
[7] "Google Maps" (http://maps.google.com.au/maps?hl=en&ie=UTF8&ll=-33.858745,151.229124&spn=0.000489,0.001404&t=h&z=20). Maps.google.com.au. 1970-01-01. . Retrieved 2011-10-30.
[8] "New Town v. Cricketers" (http://trove.nla.gov.au/ndp/del/article/8977724). *The Mercury*. 1879-06-09. . Retrieved 2011-07-26.
[9] "Balgownie Rangers Soccer Club – Club History" (http://web.archive.org/web/20060824063128/http://www.balgownierangers.com.au/history/history.htm). 2006. Archived from the original (http://www.balgownierangers.com.au/history/history.htm) on 24 August 2006. . Retrieved 4 December 2006.
[10] "Athletics Australia - History" (http://www.athletics.com.au/inside/history). Athletics.com.au. . Retrieved 2011-10-30.
[11] by J. G. Williams. "Biography - Richmond Theophilus (Dick) Cavill - Australian Dictionary of Biography" (http://adbonline.anu.edu.au/biogs/A070720b.htm). Adbonline.anu.edu.au. . Retrieved 2011-10-30.
[12] "AFL History" (http://www.afl.com.au/development/aflexplained/history/tabid/10296/default.aspx). Afl.com.au. . Retrieved 2011-10-30.
[13] "Badminton Australia - History of Badminton in Australia" (http://www.badminton.org.au/index.php?id=37). Badminton.org.au. . Retrieved 2011-10-30.
[14] "Australian Judo Federation - History" (http://www.ausjudo.com.au/jfa/jsp/read_more/read_more.jsp?title=History&read_more_id=col_2_readmorehttp://www.ausjudo.com.au/./jfa/global). Ausjudo.com.au. . Retrieved 2011-10-30.
[15] Department of Sport, Recreation and Tourism; Australian Sport Commission (1985). *Australian Sport, a profile*. Canberra, Australia: Australian Government Publish Service. p. 184. ISBN 0644036672.
[16] Evening Post (19 December 1922). "Women in Print" (http://paperspast.natlib.govt.nz/cgi-bin/paperspast?a=d&cl=search&d=EP19221219.2.83&srpos=3&e=-------10--1----0Netball+South+Africa--). *Evening Post* (New Zealand: National Library of New Zealand) **CC** (147): p. 19. . Retrieved 28 April 2011.
[17] "Australian Diving Hall of Fame" (http://www.diving.asn.au/default.asp?MenuID=About_Us/20002/1785/,Hall_of_Fame/20011/1827/). Diving.asn.au. . Retrieved 2011-10-30.
[18] Stell, Marion K. (1991). *Half the Race, A history of Australian women in sport*. North Ryde, Australia: Harper Collins. p. 100. ISBN 0207169713.
[19] MenuID=AC_Information/93/0/,Australian_Canoeing_History/69/0/ Canoeing and Kayaking Australia - History (http://www.canoe.org.au/default.asp?)
[20] "Canoeing and Kayaking Australia - Olympic history" (http://www.canoe.org.au/). Canoe.org.au. 2009-02-15. . Retrieved 2011-10-30.
[21] "Athletics Australia - Annual Report 2006/07" (http://www.athletics.com.au/inside/athletics_australia/annual_reports/2006_2007). Athletics.com.au. . Retrieved 2011-10-30.
[22] "More chase Sherrin than before" (http://realfooty.com.au/news/news/we-love-aussie-rules/2007/06/19/1182019117471.html). realfooty.com.au. . Retrieved 2011-10-30.
[23] "Basketball numbers are booming in Geelong - Local News - Geelong, VIC, Australia" (http://www.geelongadvertiser.com.au/article/2010/07/01/187051_geelong_sports.html). Geelongadvertiser.com.au. 2010-07-01. . Retrieved 2011-10-30.
[24] "Basketball popularity exploding across Melbourne's fringe" (http://www.heraldsun.com.au/news/victoria/basketball-is-most-popular-sport/story-e6frf7kx-1225884928551). Herald Sun. 2010-06-28. . Retrieved 2011-10-30.
[25] "World Cup soccer fans abandon reality for fantasy, says Neil Mitchell" (http://www.heraldsun.com.au/opinion/just-a-soccer-ruse/story-e6frfhqf-1225886397854). Herald Sun. 2010-07-01. . Retrieved 2011-10-30.
[26] Australian Bureau of Statistics catalogue no. 4177.0 - Participation in Sports and Physical Recreation, Australia, 2005-06
[27] "Surf lifesaving" (http://culture.gov.au/articles/surflifesaving/). Culture.gov.au. 2008-02-26. . Retrieved 2011-10-30.
[28] "Web Archive Copy: Sports Factor: Amateurism in Sport" (http://www.ausport.gov.au/fulltext/2002/sportsf/s488161.asp). Ausport.gov.au. 2002-02-22. . Retrieved 2011-10-30.
[29] For 1998/1999 data, the number used is the ABS corrected participation rate.
[30] National Centre for Culture and Recreation Statistics, Australian Bureau of Statistics (July 2002). *Sport Data on Participation and Attendance: How do Results from the Australian Bureau of Statistics and Sweeney Research Compare?* (http://fulltext.ausport.gov.au/fulltext/2001/abs/abssweeney.pdf). Adelaide: Australian Sport Commission. p. 10. .
[31] IBAF (http://www.baseball.ch/2003/f/mc/mcAUS.html)
[32] "Basketball in Australia" (http://www.nbl.com.au/index.php?id=959). National Basketball League. . Retrieved 4 October 2011.

[33] "Gymnastics Australia website" (http://gymnastics.org.au/). Gymnastics.org.au. . Retrieved 2011-10-30.
[34] "Sporting Shooters Association of Australia website" (http://www.ssaa.org.au/). Ssaa.org.au. . Retrieved 2011-10-30.
[35] de Bourg, Ross, "The Australian and New Zealand Thoroughbred", Nelson, West Melbourne, 1980, ISBN 0170058603
[36] "Cardigan Bay" (http://www.teara.govt.nz/TheSettledLandscape/IntroducedPlantsAndAnimals/Horses/8/ENZ-Resources/Standard/3/en). . Retrieved 3 June 2009.
[37] Shaun Amauri Moran says: (2009-10-25). "A-League Suffering Attendance Decline" (http://www.insidefutbol.com/2009/10/25/australian-a-league-suffering-attendance-decline/11426/). Insidefutbol.com. . Retrieved 2011-10-30.
[38] AFL, "All-time attendance record for 2008" (29 September 2008) (http://www.afl.com.au/News/NEWSARTICLE/tabid/208/Default.aspx?newsId=68430) Access date: 30 September 2008.
[39] "Attendance Record" (http://www.nrl.com/news/news/newsarticle/tabid/10874/newsid/60086/telstra-premiership-sets-new-attendance-record/default.aspx). *National Rugby League*. .
[40] "Statistics » Attendance » 2010-11" (http://www.ultimatealeague.com/records.php?type=att&season=2010-11). Ultimate A-League. . Retrieved 2011-10-30.
[41] "2011 AFL Crowds and Match Attendances" (http://www.footywire.com/afl/footy/attendances?year=2011&t=A&h=A&s=A). Footywire.com. . Retrieved 2011-10-30.
[42] Racing Fact Book (http://www.australianracingboard.com.au/factbook/07_08_factbook/arbFinalBook.PDF)
[43] "Rugby League Tables / Attendances" (http://stats.rleague.com/rl/crowds/summary.html). Stats.rleague.com. . Retrieved 2011-10-30.
[44] "Rugby League Tables / State Of Origin" (http://stats.rleague.com/rl/soo/soo_idx.html). Stats.rleague.com. . Retrieved 2011-10-30
[45] "Sport and the media" (http://australia.gov.au/about-australia/australian-story/sport-and-the-media). Australian Government. 15 February 2008. . Retrieved 5 October 2011.
[46] Masters, Roy (4 October 2009). "Messenger can watch a better league broadcast in the US than south of the border" (http://www.brisbanetimes.com.au/business/messenger-can-watch-a-better-league-broadcast-in-the-us-than-south-of-the-border-20091004-ghve.html). *Brisbane Times*. Fairfax Digital. . Retrieved 4 October 2011.
[47] "Keep Sport Free: The Facts" (http://www.keepsportfree.com.au/Content_Common/pg-the-facts.seo). . Retrieved 4 October 2011.
[48] "Free to Air TV Ratings, Sunday October 9, 2011" (http://www.throng.com.au/ratings/free-air-tv-ratings-october-9th-2011). 11 October 2011. .
[49] "Free to Air TV Ratings, Sunday October 2, 2011" (http://www.throng.com.au/ratings/free-air-tv-ratings-sunday-october-2-2011). 3 October 2011. . Retrieved 4 October 2011.
[50] "Free to Air TV Ratings, Saturday October 1, 2011" (http://www.throng.com.au/ratings/free-air-tv-ratings-saturday-october-1-2011). 2 October 2011. . Retrieved 4 October 2011.
[51] "Free to Air TV Ratings, Thursday September 29, 2011" (http://www.throng.com.au/ratings/free-air-tv-ratings-thursday-september-29-2011). 30 September 2011. . Retrieved 4 October 2011.
[52] "Free to Air TV Ratings, Sunday September 25, 2011" (http://www.throng.com.au/ratings/free-air-tv-ratings-sunday-september-25-2011). 26 September 2011. . Retrieved 4 October 2011.
[53] "Free to Air TV Ratings, Monday September 26, 2011" (http://www.throng.com.au/ratings/free-air-tv-ratings-monday-september-26-2011). 27 September 2011. . Retrieved 4 October 2011.
[54] "Free to Air TV Ratings, Saturday September 24, 2011" (http://www.throng.com.au/ratings/free-air-tv-ratings-saturday-september-24-2011). 25 September 2011. . Retrieved 4 October 2011.
[55] Newstalk ZB (2009-12-21). "League becomes Australia's top sport" (http://tvnz.co.nz/rugby-league-news/league-becomes-australia-s-top-sport-3315931). *TVNZ* (New Zealand: Television New Zealand Limited). . Retrieved 24 December 2009.
[56] Newstalk ZB (2009-12-21). "League becomes Australia's top sport" (http://tvnz.co.nz/rugby-league-news/league-becomes-australia-s-top-sport-3315931). *TVNZ* (New Zealand: Television New Zealand Limited). . Retrieved 2009-12-24.
[57] Canning, Simon (21 March 2011). "NRL disputes AFL audience claim" (http://www.theaustralian.com.au/business/media/nrl-disputes-afl-audience-claim/story-e6frg996-1226025045416). *The Australian*. . Retrieved 4 October 2011.
[58] Byrnes, Holly (2010-04-28). "Origin to kick-off 3D revolution" (http://www.heraldsun.com.au/sport/nrl/origin-to-kick-off-3d-revolution/story-e6frfgbo-1225859053250). *The Daily Telegraph* (Australia: Herald and Weekly Times). . Retrieved 2010-04-28.
[59] "3D State of Origin approved, World Cup announcement expected" (http://www.tvtonight.com.au/2010/05/3d-state-of-origin-approved-world-cup-announcement-expected.html). TV Tonight. 2010-05-14. . Retrieved 2011-10-30.
[60] "Studies of Australian Drama - David Williamson : The Club" (http://web.archive.org/web/20060113061720/http://www.currency.com.au/newsite/preview/club.htm). Web.archive.org. 2006-01-13. Archived from the original (http://www.currency.com.au/newsite/preview/club.htm) on 2006-01-13. . Retrieved 2011-10-30.
[61] "The Club" (http://www.rottentomatoes.com/m/1004389-club/about.php). Rotten Tomatoes. 2010-03-28. . Retrieved 2011-10-30.
[62] Daniel Williams (31 August 2007). "Footy for Thought" (http://www.time.com/time/magazine/article/0,9171,1657920,00.html). *Time* (Time Inc.). . Retrieved 2 October 2010.
[63] "At the Movies Review" (http://www.abc.net.au/atthemovies/txt/s2004682.htm). *At the Movies*, ABC. . Retrieved 29 August 2007.
[64] "Roy and HG (comedians) : programmes and related material collected by the National Library of Australia" (http://nla.gov.au/nla.cat-vn3530763). National Library of Australia (Australian performing arts collection). . Retrieved 2009-04-09.
[65] "Company Profile" (http://www.2ky.com.au/company/profile.php). 2KY (http://www.2ky.com.au). 2008. . Retrieved 2008-07-01.

[66] "Press release" (http://www.roymorgan.com/news/press-releases/2006/489/). .
[67] "AFL Record - Online Edition" (http://www.aflrecord.com.au/displayrecord/id/6). Slattery Media, Issuu. . Retrieved 5 April 2009.
[68] Matt Warshaw (2005). *The Encyclopedia of Surfing* (http://books.google.com.au/books?id=-DWQSYRx4MUC&printsec=frontcover&dq=Matt+Warshaw.+The+Encyclopedia+of+Surfing&client=firefox-a&sig=ACfU3U2d4wIqzXnglyI-d7RcxDjm2u8lig#PPA1,M1). p. 646. .
[69] Athletics Australia selection criteria (http://www.athletics.com.au/community/392/general_selection)
[70] "Australian Olympic Committee: Swimming" (http://corporate.olympics.com.au/sport/1/14/Swimming). Corporate.olympics.com.au. . Retrieved 2011-10-30.
[71] "FIFA World Cup Bracket" (http://fifaworldcup.yahoo.com/06/en/w/bracket.html). .
[72] "Seven & SBS to Broadcast Beijing Olympics" (http://www.sportbusiness.com/news/161653/seven-sbs-to-broadcast-beijing-olympics). SportBusiness. 2007-04-04. . Retrieved 2007-06-28.
[73] "Who are the Qantas Wallabies?" (http://www.rugby.com.au/qantas_wallabies/brief_history/who_are_the_wallabies,143.html). Australian Rugby Union. . Retrieved 2009-03-28.
[74] "Wallaroos: History" (http://aru.rugby.com.au/fixtures_results/wallaroos/history,47922.html). Australian Rugby Union. . Retrieved 2007-11-23.
[75] "Paper to Paper Wallaroos Squad -Samoa" (http://rugby.com.au/fixtures_results/wallaroos/2009_wallaroo_squad,48368.html) (Press release). Australian Rugby Union. . Retrieved 2009-07-24.
[76] Fagan, Sean (2 December 2009). "The Kangaroos Mascot" (http://www.webcitation.org/5s1iExUHK). rl1908.com. Archived from the original (http://www.rl1908.com/Kangaroos/badge.htm) on 2010-08-16. . Retrieved 2010-08-16.
[77] Fagan, Sean. "The Australian Rugby League Kangaroos" (http://www.webcitation.org/5s1i6Eq3o). RL1908.com. Archived from the original (http://www.rl1908.com/arlkangaroos.htm) on 2010-08-16. . Retrieved 2007-11-23.
[78] "VB Kangaroos squad named" (http://www.nrl.com/vb-kangaroos-squad-named/tabid/10874/newsid/65111/default.aspx). NRL.com. . Retrieved 2011-11-24.
[79] ARL (2008). "Jillaroos gunning for a spot in World Cup final" (http://www.webcitation.org/5s1jNunuU). Archived from the original (http://www.australianrugbyleague.com.au/news/article.php?id=1258) on 2010-08-16. . Retrieved 2010-08-16.
[80] "Australian Women's Rugby League - the online home of the Jillaroos" (http://awrljillaroos.leaguenet.com.au/). . Retrieved 2008-01-18.
[81] Australian Athletes with a Disability (October - November 2007). "Australian Athletes with a Disability Newsletter" (http://www.sports.org.au/newsletters/oct_nov2007.html) (Press release). . Retrieved 2007-11-22. "The Steelers, Australia's National Wheelchair Rugby team, recently competed in the cross Tasman Chris Handy Cup challenge"
[82] AAP Sports News (15 September 2004). "Wheelabies challenged by disability rating change" (http://www.highbeam.com/doc/1P1-99041750.html). . Retrieved 2007-11-22. "The Australian wheelchair rugby team's bid for gold in Athens has suffered a major blow [...]"
[83] Overington, Caroline (30 October 2000). "Paralympics 2000: Hero Hucks not enough". *The Age*. "Australia (which calls itself the Steelers but for whom the popular name is the Wheelabies)"
[84] "National Teams" (http://www.footballaustralia.com.au/Australia/default.aspx?s=australia). Football Federation Australia. . Retrieved 2007-11-23.
[85] "Qantas Futsalroos undone by hosts" (http://www.footballaustralia.com.au/Community/default.aspx?s=community_newsfeatures_news_news_item&id=22192). Football Federation Australia. 15 May 2008. . Retrieved 2008-08-20.
[86] "Astros & the Outback" (http://www.astros.canberra.net.au/ahistory.shtml). Astros Gridiron Football Club. . Retrieved 2008-01-21.
[87] "Gridiron History in Aus" (http://www.astros.canberra.net.au/outback.shtml). Astros Gridiron Football Club. 1999. . Retrieved 2008-01-21.
[88] "Australian netball team named the Diamonds" (http://www.abc.net.au/news/stories/2008/09/08/2358438.htm). ABC News. 8 September 2008. . Retrieved 2008-10-29.
[89] "TELSTRA AUSTRALIAN DOLPHINS SQUADS" (http://web.archive.org/web/20070904195925/http://swimming.org.au/upload/swimming+australia/high+performance/selection+criteria/2007+telstra+dolphins+squad+criteria+v2.pdf) (PDF). Swimming Australia. 2007. Archived from the original (http://www.swimming.org.au/upload/swimming australia/high performance/selection criteria/2007 telstra dolphins squad criteria v2.pdf) on 2007-09-04. . Retrieved 2007-11-23.
[90] "Australian Open Men's team" (http://www.softball.org.au/default.asp?Page=24756&MenuID=National_Teams/4019/0). Softball Australia. 2008. . Retrieved 2008-08-20.
[91] "Open Women's Team - Aussie Spirit" (http://www.softball.org.au/default.asp?Page=21993&MenuID=Teams/4019/0). Softball Australia. 2006. . Retrieved 2008-08-20.
[92] "Aussie Sharks win historic bronze medal at World League Super Finals" (http://www.australianwaterpolo.com.au/content/view/375/2/). Australian Water Polo. 12 August 2007. . Retrieved 2007-11-23.
[93] "Basketball Australia Annual Report" (http://www.basketball.net.au/_uploads/res/1_39264.pdf.) (PDF). Basketball Australia. 2006. . Retrieved 2007-11-23.
[94] "Toshiba and Cycling Australia - The Perfect Team" (http://www.cycling.org.au/default.asp?id=9292). Cycling Australia. 5 November 2007. . Retrieved 2008-08-20.
[95] "National Teams" (http://web.archive.org/web/20071103095927/http://www.hockey.org.au/Default.aspx?tabid=71). Hockey Australia. Archived from the original (http://www.hockey.org.au/Default.aspx?tabid=71) on 2007-11-03. . Retrieved 2007-11-23.

[96] "All that you ever wanted to know about hockey in and around Australia." (http://www.playinghockey.com.au/). playinghockey.com.au. 2006. . Retrieved 2008-01-15. "There are four national hockey teams in Australia, Kookaburras Australian Men's Hockey Team, Hockeyroos is the Australian Women's Hockey Team, Jillaroos is the Australian Under 21 Women's Team and Burras is the Australian Under 21 Men's Team."
[97] "2004 ANZ HOCKEYROOS SQUAD" (http://web.archive.org/web/20070829214605/http://www.hockey.org.au/Default. aspx?tabid=293). Hockey Australia. Archived from the original (http://www.hockey.org.au/Default.aspx?tabid=293) on 2007-08-29. . Retrieved 2007-11-23.
[98] Rurak, Don (January 2004). "From the President: Newsletter" (http://www.iha.org.au/president_news_jan04.asp) (Press release). Ice Hockey Australia. . Retrieved 2007-11-23. "Adoption of the "Mighty Roos" name, logo and jersey for the Australian Senior Men's National Team."
[99] Koreen, Mike (16 May 2003). "Green Aussies grin and bear it; Box lacrosse underdogs are giving it their all". *The Toronto Sun*: p. Sports, p.81. "They produced some t-shirts with the team's nickname — Boxaroos — printed on them."
[100] "Jackaroos is a winner" (http://www.bowls-aust.com.au/cp1/c2/webi/externaldocument/00000824aai.htm). Bowls Australia. August 2004. . "As a result, the Australian men's bowls team has a new nickname - the Jackaroos. [...] The jackaroo is symbolic of the Australian outback. And the first part of the word - jack - is the most common name for the small white ball that is the prime focus and target in a game of bowls."
[101] "The shining Sapphires" (http://web.archive.org/web/20070830002645/http://www.bowlsaustralia.com.au/default. asp?pg=default&spg=display&articleid=37535). Bowls Australia. 2004. Archived from the original (http://www.bowlsaustralia.com.au/default.asp?pg=default&spg=display&articleid=37535) on 2007-08-30. . Retrieved 2007-11-23. "After much deliberation the new nickname for the Australian women's bowls team is the Sapphires."
[102] "Orienteer: Aussie team to be called Boomerangs" (http://findarticles.com/p/articles/mi_7235/is_200608/ai_n30555347). AAP. 2 August 2006. . Retrieved 2009-03-09.
[103] Valerino, John (20 September 2000). "What's in a nickname anyway?". *The Ledger*: p. C1.
[104] "Women's handball rookie set for world championships" (http://www.bhtafe.edu.au/News/newsHandballChampion.htm). Box Hill Institute. 12 October 2005. . Retrieved 2009-03-09.
[105] "Australian Flying Disc Association 2008 Annual Report" (http://www.afda.com/resources/2008AFDAAnnualReport.pdf). AFDA. . Retrieved 20 April 2011.
[106] Howell, Max; Howell, Reet; Brown, David W. (1989). *The Sporting Image, A pictorial history of Queenslanders at play*. Brisbane: University of Queensland Press. p. 84. ISBN 0702222062.
[107] Taylor, Tracy (1998). "Issues of cultural diversity in women's sport" (http://wopared.parl.net/Senate/committee/ecita_ctte/completed_inquiries/2004-07/womeninsport/submissions/sub29att5.pdf). *Women in Sport*. **29**. p. 6. . Retrieved 28 February 2011.
[108] Van Bottenburg 2001, p. 214
[109] DaCosta & Miragaya 2002, p. 66
[110] Department of Foreign Affairs and Trade (May 2008). "About Australia: Sporting Events" (http://www.dfat.gov.au/facts/sporting_events.html). . Retrieved 3 March 2011.
[111] "Missing chair provides Paralympic scare" (http://news.smh.com.au/sport/missing-chair-provides-paralympic-scare-20080902-47n2.html). 2008-09-02. . Retrieved 2008-09-03.
[112] Murdoch, Alex (2008-09-05). "Beijing Paralympics lose friendly tone in gold hunt" (http://www.news.com.au/couriermail/story/0,23739,24294775-10389,00.html). *The Courier-Mail*. . Retrieved 2008-09-04.
[113] Athletes: Vancouver 2010 Winter Paralympics (http://www.vancouver2010.com/paralympic-games/athletes/), The Official Website of the Vancouver 2010 Olympic and Paralympic Winter Games
[114] "Paralympic Games History – Winter" (http://en.wikipedia.org/wiki/Wikipedia:Sockpuppet_investigations/Seksen_iki_yÃ¼z_kÄ±rk_beÅ). Australian Paralympic Committee. . Retrieved 9 June 2011.

References

Further reading

- Marschik, Matthias. "Austrian Sport and the Challenges of Its Recent Historiography," *Journal of Sport History*, Summer 2011, Vol. 38 Issue 2, pp 189-198

External links

- Australian Sports Commission (http://www.ausport.gov.au)
- Australian Institute of Sport (http://www.ais.org.au)

Northern Territory

Northern Territory	

Flag	
Slogan or nickname: *The Territory, The NT, The Top End*	
Motto(s): *none*	
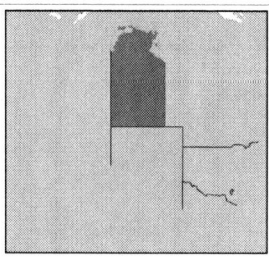	
Other Australian states and territories	
Capital	Darwin
Demonym	Territorian
Government	Constitutional monarchy
- Administrator	Sally Thomas
- Chief Minister	Paul Henderson (ALP)
Australian Territory	
- Established by NSW	1825
- Transferred to South Australia	1863
- Transferred to Commonwealth	1911
- Dissolved	1927
- Reformed	1931
- Responsible Government	1978
Area	
- Total	1420970 km² (3rd) 548640 sq mi
- Land	1349129 km² 520902 sq mi
- Water	71839 km² (5.06%) 27737 sq mi
Population (June 2010)	
- Population	229,675 (8th)

- Density	0.17/km² (8th) 0.4 /sq mi
Elevation	
- Highest	Mount Zeil +1,531 m (5,023 ft)
Gross Territorial Product (2009–10)	
- Product ($m)	$16,880[1] (8th)
- Product per capita	$73,495 (2nd)
Time zone	ACST UTC+9:30 does not observe DST
Federal representation	
- House seats	2
- Senate seats	2
Abbreviations	
- Postal	NT
- ISO 3166-2	AU-NT
Emblems	
- Floral	Sturt's Desert Rose
- Animal	Red Kangaroo
- Bird	Wedge-tailed Eagle
- Colours	Black, white, and ochre
Web site	www.nt.gov.au [2]

The **Northern Territory** is a federal territory of Australia, occupying much of the centre of the mainland continent, as well as the central northern regions. It shares borders with Western Australia to the west (129th meridian east), South Australia to the south (26th parallel south), and Queensland to the east (138th meridian east).

To the north, the territory is bordered by the Timor Sea, the Arafura Sea and the Gulf of Carpentaria. Despite its large area—over 1349129 square kilometres (sq mi), making it the third largest Australian federal division—it is sparsely populated. With a population of 229,675 it is the least populous of Australia's eight major states and territories.[3]

The archeological history of the Northern Territory begins over 40,000 years ago when Indigenous Australians settled the region. Makassan traders began trading with the indigenous people of the Northern Territory for trepang from at least the 18th century onwards, and very likely for 300 years prior to that.

The coast of the territory was first seen by Europeans in the 17th century. The British were the first Europeans to attempt to settle the coastal regions in the 19th century; however no attempt was successful until the establishment of a settlement at Port Darwin in 1869. Today the economy is based on tourism, especially Kakadu National Park in the Top End and the Uluru-Kata Tjuta National Park (Ayers Rock) in central Australia, and mining.

The capital city is Darwin. The population is not concentrated in coastal regions but rather along the Stuart Highway. The other major settlements are (in order of size) Alice Springs, Katherine, Nhulunbuy, and Tennant Creek.

Residents of the Northern Territory are often known simply as 'Territorians'.

History

Indigenous Australians have lived in the present area of the Northern Territory for an estimated 40,000 years, and extensive seasonal trade links existed between them and the peoples of what is now Indonesia for at least five centuries.

With the coming of the British, there were four early attempts to settle the harsh environment of the northern coast, of which three failed in starvation and despair. The Northern Territory was part of New South Wales from 1825 to 1863, except for a brief time from February to December 1846, when it was part of the short lived colony of North Australia. It was part of South Australia from 1863 to 1911. Under the administration of South Australia, the overland telegraph was constructed between 1870 and 1872.

A railway was also built between Palmerston and Pine Creek between 1883 and 1889. The economic pattern of cattle raising and mining was established so that by 1911 there were 513,000 cattle. Victoria River Downs was at one time the largest cattle station in the world. Gold was found at Grove Hill in 1872 and at Pine Creek, Brocks Creek, Burrundi, and copper was found at Daly River.

Thomas Baines with Aborigines near the mouth of the Victoria River.

On 1 January 1911, a decade after federation, the Northern Territory was separated from South Australia and transferred to Commonwealth control. Alfred Deakin opined at this time "To me the question has been not so much commercial as national, first, second, third and last. Either we must accomplish the peopling of the northern territory or submit to its transfer to some other nation."

In late 1912 there was growing sentiment that the name "Northern Territory" was unsatisfactory.[4][5] The names "Kingsland" (after King George V and to correspond with Queensland), "Centralia" and "Territoria" were proposed with Kingsland becoming the preferred choice in 1913. However, the name change never went ahead.[6][7]

For a brief time between 1927 and 1931 the Northern Territory was divided into North Australia and Central Australia at the 20th parallel of South latitude. Soon after this time, parts of the Northern Territory were considered in the Kimberley Plan as a possible site for the establishment of a Jewish Homeland, understandably considered the "Unpromised Land".

During World War II, most of the Top End was placed under military government. This is the only time since Federation that an Australian state or territory has been under military control. After the war, control for the entire area was handed back to the Commonwealth.

Letters Patent annexing the Northern Territory to South Australia, 1863

Indigenous Australians had struggled for rights to fair wages and land. An important event in this struggle was the strike and walk off by the Gurindji people at Wave Hill Cattle Station in 1966. The Commonwealth Government of Gough Whitlam set up the Woodward Royal Commission in February 1973, which set to inquire into how land rights might be achieved in the Northern Territory. Justice Woodward's first report in July 1973 recommended that a

Central Land Council and a Northern Land Council be established in order to present to him the views of Aboriginal people. In response to the report of the Royal Commission a Land Rights Bill was drafted, but the Whitlam Government was dismissed before it was passed.

The Aboriginal Land Rights (Northern Territory) Act 1976 was eventually passed by the Fraser Government on 16 December 1976 and began operation on the following Australia Day (26 January 1977).

In 1978 the Territory was granted responsible government, with a Legislative Assembly headed by a Chief Minister.

During 1996 the Northern Territory was briefly one of the few places in the world with legal voluntary euthanasia, until the Federal Parliament overturned the legislation.[8] Before the overriding legislation was enacted, three people committed suicide through voluntary euthanasia, a practice orchestrated by Dr. Philip Nitschke.

Geography

There are many very small settlements scattered across the territory, but the larger population centres are located on the single paved road that links Darwin to southern Australia, the Stuart Highway, known to locals simply as "the track".

The Northern Territory is also home to two spectacular natural rock formations, Uluru (Ayers Rock) and Kata Tjuta (The Olgas), which are sacred to the local Aboriginal peoples and which have become major tourist attractions.

In the northern part of the territory lies Kakadu National Park, which features breathtaking wetlands and native wildlife. To the north of that lies the Arafura Sea, and to the east lies Arnhem Land, whose regional centre is Maningrida on the Liverpool River delta. There is an extensive series of river systems in the Northern Territory. These rivers include: the Alligator Rivers, Daly River, Finke River, McArthur River, Roper River, Todd River and Victoria River.

Northern Territory towns, settlements and road network.

National parks

- Arnhem Land (Restricted Area)
- Barranyi Nth. Island National Park
- Casuarina Coastal Reserve
- Daly River Nature Park
- Devils Marbles Conservation Reserve
- Djukbinj National Park
- Elsey National Park

- Finke Gorge National Park
- Gregory National Park
- Gurig National Park-now Garig Gunak Barlu National Park
- Howard Springs Nature Park Conservation Reserve
- Kakadu National Park
- Keep River National Park
- Litchfield National Park
- Mary River Crossing Conservation Reserve and proposed Mary River National Park
- Mataranka Thermal Springs
- Nitmiluk National Park
  - Katherine Gorge
- Palm Valley
- Tanami Desert
  - The Olgas
- Uluru-Kata Tjuta National Park
- Watarrka National Park (including Kings Canyon)
- West MacDonnell National Park

Mount Sonder, the fourth highest mountain in the Northern Territory after nearby Mount Zeil, in West MacDonnell National Park.

Nourlangie Rock in Kakadu National Park.

Uluru, (Ayers Rock) one of the best known images of the Northern Territory.

Climate

Satellite image of fire activity in central Australia.

Average monthly maximum temperature in Northern Territory		
Month	Darwin	Alice Springs
January	31.8 °C	36.3 °C
February	31.4 °C	35.1 °C
March	31.9 °C	32.7 °C
April	32.7 °C	28.2 °C
May	32.0 °C	23.0 °C
June	30.6 °C	19.8 °C
July	30.5 °C	19.7 °C
August	31.3 °C	22.6 °C
September	32.5 °C	27.1 °C
October	33.2 °C	30.9 °C
November	33.2 °C	33.7 °C
December	33.6 °C	35.4 °C
Source: Bureau of Meteorology		

The Northern Territory has two distinctive climate zones.

The northern end, including Darwin, has a tropical climate with high humidity and two seasons, the wet (November to April) and dry season (May to October). During the dry season nearly every day is warm and sunny, and afternoon humidity averages around 30%. There is very little rainfall between May and September. In the coolest months of June and July, the daily minimum temperature may dip as low as 14 °C (57 °F), but very rarely lower, and frost has never been recorded.

The wet season is associated with tropical cyclones and monsoon rains. The majority of rainfall occurs between December and March (the southern hemisphere summer), when thunderstorms are common and afternoon relative humidity averages over 70% during the wettest months. On average more than 1570 mm (62 in) of rain falls in the north. Rainfall is highest in north west coastal areas, where rainfall averages from 1,800–2,100mm.

The central region is the desert centre of the country, which includes Alice Springs and Ayers Rock, and is semi-arid with little rain usually falling during the hottest months from October to March. Central Australia receives less than 250 mm (9.8 in) of rain per year.

The highest temperature recorded in the territory was 48.3 °C (118.9 °F) at Finke on 1 and 2 January 1960. The lowest temperature was −7.5 °C (18.5 °F) at Alice Springs on 12 July 1976.[9]

Governance

Parliament

The Northern Territory Parliament is one of the three unicameral parliaments in the country. Based on the Westminster System, it consists of the Northern Territory Legislative Assembly which was created in 1974, replacing the Northern Territory Legislative Council.

The Northern Territory Legislative Council was the partly elected governing body from 1947 until its replacement by the fully elected Northern Territory Legislative Assembly in 1974. The total enrolment for the 1947 election was 4,443, all of whom were white. The Northern Territory was split into five electorates: Darwin, Alice Springs, Tennant Creek, Batchelor, and Stuart.

The legislative assembly building in Darwin.

Whilst this assembly exercises similar powers as the governments of the states of Australia, it does so by legislated delegation of powers from the Commonwealth Government, rather than by any constitutional right. The Monarch is represented by the Administrator of the Northern Territory which is similar to that of state governors.

Twenty-five members of the Legislative Assembly are elected to four-year terms from single-member electorates.

For several years there has been agitation for full statehood. A referendum was held on the issue in 1998, which resulted in a 'no' vote. This was a shock to both the Northern Territory and Commonwealth governments, for opinion polls showed most Territorians supported statehood. However, under the Australian Constitution, the Federal Government may set the terms of entry to full statehood. The Northern Territory was offered three Senators, rather than the twelve guaranteed to original states. (Because of the difference in populations, equal numbers of Senate seats would mean a Territorian's vote for a Senator would have been worth more than 30 votes in New South Wales or Victoria.) Alongside what was cited as an arrogant approach adopted by then Chief Minister Shane Stone, it is believed that most Territorians, regardless of their general views on statehood, were reluctant to adopt the particular offer that was made.[10]

Chief Minister and Cabinet

The Chief Minister of the Northern Territory is the head of government of a self-governing territory, while the head of government of a state is a Premier. The Chief Minister is appointed by the Administrator of the Northern Territory, who in normal circumstances will appoint the head of whatever party holds the majority of seats in the Northern Territory Legislative Assembly. The current Chief Minister of the Northern Territory is Paul Henderson.

Paul Henderson replaced Clare Martin on 26 November 2007. The Leader of the Opposition was Denis Burke, head of the Country Liberal Party, until the Territory elections of June 2005, where Burke lost his seat. The party then chose Terry Mills as the new Opposition Leader. Subsequently, Jodeen Carney took over for a time. In January 2008, Terry Mills again became the Opposition Leader.

Administrator

The Northern Territory received self-government on 1 July 1978 under its own Administrator of the Northern Territory appointed by the Governor-General of Australia. The Commonwealth government, not the Government of the Northern Territory, advises the governor-general on appointment of the Administrator, but by convention, consults first with the Territory Government. The current administrator, Tom Pauling, was sworn in on 9 November 2007.

Federal government

The Northern Territory is represented in the Commonwealth parliament by two Members in the House of Representatives, currently Warren Snowdon from the Australian Labor Party (ALP) and Natasha Griggs from the Country Liberal Party (CLP), and two members in the Senate, currently Trish Crossin for the ALP and Nigel Scullion for the CLP.

Local government

The Northern Territory is divided into 17 Local Government Areas, including 11 shires and five municipalities. Shire, city and town councils are responsible for functions delegated by the Northern Territory parliament, such as city planning, road infrastructure and waste management. Council revenue comes mostly from property taxes and government grants.

Aboriginal land councils

Further information: Aboriginal land councils in the Northern Territory

Aboriginal land councils in the Northern Territory are areas of Aboriginal self-governance.

Demographics

Northern Territory population by year	
1901	4,765
1956	19,556
1961	44,481
1974	102,924
1975	92,869
1981	122,616
1991	165,493
2002	199,411

2006	210,600
2011	230,200
2021	296,300
2031	364,000
2056	573,000
Source: Australian Bureau of Statistics	

Darwin skyline from East Point

The population of the Northern Territory in late 2006 was estimated at 212,600[11] This was an 1.8% increase from the 2001 Australian Bureau of Statistics report, and the population represents 1% of the total population of Australia.

The estimated population of the Northern Territory at the end of 2008 was 221,100. The population grew 2.2% which was the second largest growth in the country with Queensland after Western Australia which grew 2.4%.

The Northern Territory's population is the youngest in Australia and has the largest proportion under 15 years of age and the smallest proportion aged 65 and over. The median age of residents of the Northern Territory is 30.3 years, almost six years younger than the national median age.

More than 100 nationalities are represented in the Northern Territory's population, including more than 50 organisations representing different ethnic groups.[12]

The 2006 Census revealed that of the Northern Territory's population, 68.4% is of European descent. 64,491 (30.6%) English with 44,662 (20.2%), Irish with 14,346 (6.8%), Scottish with 11,759 (5.6%), German with 7,729 (3.7%) and Italian with 3,308 (1.5%). Indigenous Australian people make up 32.5% of the Northern Territory's population, while Chinese people with 4,081 make up (1.9%).

Indigenous Australians own some 49% of the land. The life expectancy of Aboriginal Australians is well below that of non-Indigenous Australians in the Northern Territory, a fact that is mirrored elsewhere in Australia. ABS statistics suggest that Indigenous Australians die about 11 years earlier than the average Australian. There are Aboriginal communities in many parts of the territory, the largest ones being the Pitjantjatjara near Uluru, the Arrernte near Alice Springs, the Luritja between those two, the Warlpiri further north, and the Yolngu in eastern Arnhem Land.

In terms of birthplace, according to the 2006 census 13.8% of the population were born overseas.[13] 2.6% of Territorians were born in England, 1.7% in New Zealand, 1.0% in Philippines, 0.6% in the United States and 0.5% in East Timor.

More than 54% of Territorians live in Darwin, located in the territory's north (Top End). Less than half of the territory's population live in the rural Northern Territory.

Rank	Statistical Division/District	2008–2009 Population[14]
1	**Darwin**	124,760
2	Palmerston	30,005
3	Alice Springs	27,877
4	Katherine	10,095
5	Nhulunbuy	5,001
6	Tennant Creek	3,558
7	Wadeye	2,394
8	Jabiru	1,327
9	Yulara	1,205

Religion

53.6% of Territorians describe themselves Christian. Roman Catholics form the single largest religious group in the territory with 20.3% of the Northern Territory's population, followed by Anglican (12.7%), Uniting Church (7.0%) and Lutheran (3.6%). Buddhism is the territory's largest non-Christian religion (1.4%), followed by Islam (0.5%) and Hinduism (0.2%). Around 21.9% of Territorians do not profess any religion.[15]

Education

Primary and secondary

A Northern Territory school education consists of six years of primary schooling, including one transition year, three years of middle schooling, and three years of secondary schooling. In the beginning of 2007, the Northern Territory introduced Middle School for Years 7–9 and High School for Years 10–12. Northern Territory children generally begin school at age five. On completing secondary school, students earn the Northern Territory Certificate of Education (NTCE). Students who successfully complete their secondary education also receive a tertiary entrance ranking, or ENTER score, to determine university admittance. An International Baccalaureate is offered at one school in the Territory – Kormilda College.

A campus building of Charles Darwin University.

Northern Territory schools are either publicly or privately funded. Public schools, also known as state or government schools, are funded and run directly by the Department of Employment, Education and Training.[16] Private fee-paying schools include schools run by the Catholic Church and independent schools, some elite ones similar to English public schools. Some Northern Territory Independent schools are affiliated with Protestant, Lutheran, Anglican, Greek Orthodox or Seventh-day Adventist churches, but include non church schools and an Indigenous school.

As of 2009, the Northern Territory had 151 public schools, 15 Catholic schools and 21 independent schools. 39,492 students were enrolled in schools around the Territory with 29,175 in public schools, and 9,882 in independent schools. The Northern Territory has about 4,000 full-time teachers.

Tertiary

The Northern Territory has one university. Northern Territory University (now called Charles Darwin University) enrolled its first student in 1987.[17] Charles Darwin University had about 19,000 students enrolled: about 5500 higher education students and about 13500 students on vocational education and training (VET) courses. The first tertiary institution in the territory was the Batchelor Institute of Indigenous Tertiary Education (established in mid 1960s).

Libraries

The Northern Territory Library is the Territory's research and reference library. It is responsible for collecting and preserving the Northern Territory documentary heritage and making it available through a range of programs and services. Material in the collection includes books, newspapers, magazines, journals, manuscripts, maps, pictures, objects, sound and video recordings and databases.

Economy

The Northern Territory's economy is largely driven by mining, which is concentrated on energy producing minerals, petroleum and energy and contributes around $2.5 billion to the gross state product and employs over 4,600 people. Mining accounts for 26 per cent of the gross state product in 2006–2007 compared to just 7 per cent nationally.[18]

The Ranger Uranium Mine.

The economy has continued to grow during the 2005–2006 financial year from the past two financial years. Between 2003 and 2006 the gross state product had risen from $8,670 million to $11,476 million and increase of 32.4 per cent. During the three years to 2006–2007 the Northern Territory gross state product grew by an average annual rate of 5.5 per cent.[19] Gross state product per capita in the Northern Territory ($72,496) is higher than any Australian state or territory, and is also higher than the gross domestic product per capita for Australia ($54,606). This can be attributed to the recent mining and resources boom.

The Northern Territory's exports were up 19 per cent during 2005–2006. The largest contributor to the territory's exports was: oil and gas (33.4 per cent), iron-ore (20. per cent), other manufacturing (5.9 per cent) and agriculture (4.9 per cent). Imports to the Northern Territory totalled $2,887.8 million which consisted of mainly machinery and equipment manufacturing (58.4 per cent) and petroleum, coal, chemical and associated product manufacturing (17.0 per cent).[20]

The principal mining operations are bauxite at Gove Peninsula where the production is estimated to increase 52.1 per cent to $254 million in 2007–08. Manganese at Groote Eylandt, production is estimated to increase 10.5 per cent to $1.1 billion which will be helped by the newly developed mines include Bootu Creek and Frances Creek. Gold is estimated to increase 21.7 per cent to $482 million at the Union Reefs plant. Uranium at Ranger Uranium Mine.[21]

Tourism is one of the major industries on the Northern Territory. Iconic destinations such as Uluru and Kakadu make the Northern Territory a popular destination for domestic and international travellers. Diverse landscapes, spectacular waterfalls, wide open spaces, aboriginal culture, wild and untamed wildlife, all create a unique opportunity for the visitor to immerse themselves in the natural wonder that the Northern Territory offers. Images of Uluru (Ayers Rock) are recognised around the world ensuring that Tourism in the Northern Territory will remain a vital component of its future. In 2005–06, 1.38 million people visited the Northern Territory. They stayed for 9.2 million nights and spent over $1.5 billion.

The territory is well known for being promoted with the slogan "You'll Never Never Know if you Never Never Go". This was implemented as a result of the Kennedy Review in 1992.

Transport

The Northern Territory is the most sparsely populated state or territory in Australia. From its establishment in 1869 the Port of Darwin [22] was the major Territory supply for many decades. It was damaged in the 1942 Japanese air raids and subsequently restored. In the late 1960s improved roads in adjoining States linking with the Territory, port delays and rapid economic development led to uncertainty in port and regional infrastructure development. As a result of the Commission of Enquiry established by the Administrator,[23] port working arrangements were changed, berth investment deferred and a port masterplan prepared.[24] Extension of rail transport was then not considered because of low freight volumes.

The Lasseter Highway connects Uluru to the Stuart Highway.

Despite its sparse population there is a network of sealed roads, including two National Highways, linking with adjoining States and connecting the major Territory population centres,and some other centres such as Uluru (Ayers Rock), Kakadu and Litchfield National Parks. The Stuart Highway, known as "The Track", runs north to south, connecting Darwin and Alice Springs to Adelaide. Some of the sealed roads are single lane bitumen. Many unsealed (dirt) roads connect the more remote settlements.

The Ghan, which runs across the Territory from north to south, in Alice Springs.

The Adelaide-Darwin Railway, a new standard gauge railway, connects Adelaide via Alice Springs with Darwin, replacing earlier narrow gauge railways which had a gap between Alice Springs and Birdum.

The Northern Territory was one of the few remaining places in the world with no speed restrictions on public roads. Since 1 January 2007 a default speed limit of 110 km/h applies on roads outside of urban areas (Inside urban areas of 40, 50 or 60 km/h). Speeds of up to 130 km/h are permitted on some major highways, such as the Stuart Highway.[25]

Since the introduction of a universal 130 km/h speed limit in 2006, together with the introduction of demerit (penalty) points for speeding, the Territory's road toll has risen markedly.[26]

Darwin International Airport is the major domestic and international airport for the territory. Several smaller airports are also scattered throughout the Territory and are served by smaller airlines; including Alice Springs Airport, Ayers Rock Airport, Katherine Airport and Tennant Creek Airport.

Media

Print

The Northern Territory has only one daily tabloid newspaper, News Corporation's *Northern Territory News*; the *Centralian Advocate* is circulated around the Alice Springs region twice a week. There is a Sunday tabloid newspaper, *The Sunday Territorian*. There are also five weekly *Community Newspapers*. The Northern Territory receives the national daily, *The Australian*.

Television

Metropolitan Darwin has had five broadcast television stations:

- ABC Northern Territory. Produces nightly local news at 7pm. *(digital & analogue) (callsign: ABD – Channel 6 Analogue, Channel 30 Digital)*
- SBS Northern Territory *(digital & analogue) (callsign: SBS – Channel 28 Analogue, Channel 29 Digital)*
- Seven Network/Southern Cross Television Darwin. Produces weeknightly local news updates . *(digital & analogue) (callsign: TND – Channel 34 Analogue, Channel 32 Digital)*
- Nine Network Darwin. Produces weeknightly local news from 6pm – 6.30pm. *(digital & analogue) (callsign: NTD – Channel 8 Analogue, Channel 31 Digital)*
- Network Ten/Darwin Digital Television Darwin. Receives Ten News At Five from ATV-10 in Melbourne. *(digital & analogue) (callsign: DTD – Channel 33 Digital)*

In addition, broadcasters operate digital multichannels:

- ABC2 *(carried by ABD)*
- SBS World News Channel *(carried by SBS)*
- Ten HD *(carried by DTD)*
- Nine HD *(carried by NTD)*

Regional Northern Territory has a similar availability of stations. Imparja Television is produced from Alice Springs and is available throughout most of the Northern Territory.

Radio

Darwin has radio stations on both AM and FM frequencies. ABC stations include ABC NewsRadio (102.5FM), 105.7 ABC Darwin (8DDD 105.7FM), ABC Radio National (657AM), ABC Classic FM (107.3FM) and Triple J (103.3FM). The 2 commercial stations are: Mix 104.9 (8MIX), Hot 100 (8HOT)

The leading community stations are 104.1 Territory FM and Radio Larrakia (8KNB).

The radio stations in Alice Springs are also broadcast on the AM and FM frequencies. ABC stations include Triple J (94.9FM), ABC Classic FM (97.9FM), 783 ABC Alice Springs (783AM) and ABC Radio National (99.7FM). There are two community stations in the town--CAAMA (100.5FM) and 8CCC (102.1FM). The commercial stations, which are both owned by the same company are Sun 96.9 (96.9FM) and 8HA (900AM). Two additional stations, Territory FM (98.7FM) and Radio TAB (95.9FM) are syndicated from Darwin and Brisbane respectively.

See also

- Darwin
- Crime in the Northern Territory
- Northern Territory Police

Lists:

- Highways in the Northern Territory
- Australian Aboriginal Prehistoric Sites
- Towns in the Northern Territory
- Cities in the Northern Territory
- Local Government Areas of the Northern Territory

Notes

[1] 5220.0 – Australian National Accounts: State Accounts, 2009–10 (http://www.abs.gov.au/AUSSTATS/abs@.nsf/Lookup/5220. 0Main+Features12009-10?OpenDocument).
[2] http://www.nt.gov.au/
[3] Australian Demographic Statistics June 2010 (http://www.abs.gov.au/ausstats/abs@.nsf/mf/3101.0/), Australian Bureau of Statistics, December 2010.
[4] "The Territory: Federal Policy Criticised" (http://trove.nla.gov.au/ndp/del/article/5351157). The Advertiser. 14 November 1912. .
[5] "House of Representatives" (http://trove.nla.gov.au/ndp/del/article/15375411). Sydney Morning Herald. 14 November 1912. .
[6] "Territoria or Kingsland!" (http://trove.nla.gov.au/ndp/del/article/59253861). The Register. 16 April 1913. .
[7] "Kingsland: New name for the Northern Territory" (http://trove.nla.gov.au/ndp/del/article/5396815). The Advertiser. 22 April 1913. .
[8] Federal Parliament NT Legislation, http://www.nt.gov.au/lant/parliament/committees/rotti/parldebate.shtml
[9] "Rainfall and Temperature Records: National" (http://www.bom.gov.au/climate/extreme/records/national.pdf) (PDF). Bureau of Meteorology. . Retrieved 17 November 2009.
[10] *ABC Lateline Discussion* (http://www.abc.net.au/lateline/stories/s13445.htm) (Current Affairs). Australia: Australian Broadcasting Corporation. .
[11] "3101.0 – Australian Demographic Statistics, June 2007" (http://www.abs.gov.au/ausstats/abs@.nsf/mf/3101.0/). Australian Bureau of Statistics. 2007-12-04. .
[12] "Our Different Cultures" (http://www.migration.nt.gov.au/services.cfm?ContentID=36). Northern Territory Government. 2007-06-14. .
[13] "ABS NT Quick Stats" (http://www.censusdata.abs.gov.au/ABSNavigation/prenav/ LocationSearch?locationLastSearchTerm=Northern+Territory&locationSearchTerm=Northern+Territory&newarea=7& submitbutton=View+QuickStats+>&mapdisplay=on&collection=Census&period=2006&areacode=7&geography=&method=Place+of+ Usual+Residence&productlabel=&producttype=QuickStats&topic=&navmapdisplayed=true&javascript=true&breadcrumb=PL& topholder=0&leftholder=0&currentaction=104&action=401&textversion=false&subaction=1). Australian Bureau of Statistics. 2007-06-14. .
[14] "3218.0 – Regional Population Growth, Australia, 2006–07" (http://www.abs.gov.au/AUSSTATS/abs@.nsf/DetailsPage/3218. 02007-08?OpenDocument). Australian Bureau of Statistics. .
[15] Profiles&textversion=true&navmapdisplayed=true&breadcrumb=PLD&&collection=census&period=2006&producttype=Community Profiles&#Basic Community Profile 2006 Census Community Profile Series : Northern Territory (http://www.censusdata.abs.gov.au/ ABSNavigation/prenav/ViewData?&action=404&documentproductno=7&documenttype=Details&tabname=Details&areacode=7& issue=2006&producttype=Community Profiles&&producttype=Community)
[16] Department of Employment, Education and Training, http://www.deet.nt.gov.au/education/
[17] Charles Darwin University Annual Report, http://www.cdu.edu.au/vc/annualreport.html
[18] About Minerals and Energy Department of Regional Development, Primary Industry, Fisheries and Resources (http://www.nt.gov.au/d/ Minerals_Energy/index.cfm?header=About Minerals and Energy)
[19] Northern Territory Budget (http://www.budget.nt.gov.au/papers/econ/2_economic_growth.pdf)
[20] "Northern Territory Economics" (http://www.abs.gov.au/ausstats/abs@.nsf/7d12b0f6763c78caca257061001cc588/ 9ee724f9094de980ca257384000dbaa1!OpenDocument). *Australian Bureau of Statistics*. 2007-10-31. . Retrieved 2008-07-27.
[21] Northern Territory Budget Mining and energy (http://www.budget.nt.gov.au/papers/econ/8_mining_energy.pdf)
[22] http://nt.gov.au/dpa/
[23] Report of the Commission of Enquiry into Darwin Port Operations, Northern Territory Transport and Consumer Prices, Darwin, 1972 (http://catalogue.nla.gov.au/Records/a590549)
[24] Bureau of Transport Economics, Darwin and Northern Territory Freight Transport Study, Canberra, 1977 (http://catalogue.nla.gov.au/ Record/2794315)

[25] "Northern Territory Introduces Speed Limits" (http://www.caradvice.com.au/1059/northern-territory-indtroduces-speed-limits/). CarAdvice.com.au. 2006-11-04. .
[26] "NT Opposition Proposes Scrapping Of Highway Speed Limits" (http://www.themotorreport.com.au/39904/nt-opposition-proposes-scrapping-of-highway-speed-limits/). TheMotorReport.com.au. 2009-08-18. .

References

- Hill, Ernestine. 1951. *The Territory: The classic saga of Australia's far north*. Angus & Robertson. Reprint: 1995. ISBN 0-207-18821-1
- Govan, A. (2007) Broadband debate key to NT's future. N.T. Business Review, vol. N/A, no. N/A, p. 7
- Morrison, P. (2000) a pilot implementation of internet access for remote aboriginal communities in the "Top end" Of Australia. Urban Studies, Vol. 37, No.10, pp. 1781–1792.
- Toyne, P. (2002) Northern Territory Governments Response to the House of Representatives Communications, Information Technology & the Arts Committee inquiry into Wireless Broadband Communications. In N.T. GOVERNMENT (Ed.) (pp. 3). Darwin: Northern Territory Government.
- Toyne, P. (2003) Remote Areas Telecommunications Strategy 2003–2008. In N. T. GOVERNMENT (Ed.) (pp. 1– 32). Darwin N.T. viewed 6 February 2008, <http://www.nt.gov.au/dcis/it/docs/ntg_remote_telec_strat.pdf>

External links

- Northern Territory Government of Australia (http://www.nt.gov.au/)
- Northern Territory Visitor's Guide (http://www.travelnt.com/)
- Australian Bureau of Statistics (27 April 2007). "Northern Territory at a Glance, 2007" (http://www.abs.gov.au/AUSSTATS/abs@.nsf/DetailsPage/1304.72007?OpenDocument) (PDF 855 kB).
- Northern Territory National Emergency Response Bill 2007 (http://www.nit.com.au/breakingNews/story.aspx?id=12229)
- Intervention Program in Indigenous communities and town camps (http://www.stopabuse.nt.gov.au/updates/today.shtml)
- Northern Territory Weather and Warnings Summary (http://www.bom.gov.au/nt/) from the Bureau of Meteorology
- Northern-Territory Northern Territory Climate (http://www.britannica.com/eb/article-43512/)
- Northern Territory economy/mining (http://www.nt.gov.au/dpifm/Minerals_Energy/index.cfm?header=About Minerals and Energy/)
- Northern Territory Education (http://www.deet.nt.gov.au/education/)
- Report on NT Education (http://www.deet.nt.gov.au/corporate/annual_report/2006-2007/docs/deet_annual_report_2006_07.pdf)
- Northern Territory Universities (http://www.cdu.edu.au/visiting/abouthistory.html)
- Northern Territory Population estimates June 2007 (http://www.abs.gov.au/AUSSTATS/abs@.nsf/mf/3101.0?OpenDocument)
- June 2007 NT population estimates (http://www.ausstats.abs.gov.au/ausstats/subscriber.nsf/0/26E2ADC6E07B7A12CA2573A6001351D2/$File/31010_jun 2007.pdf)

Article Sources and Contributors

Sport in the Northern Territory *Source*: http://en.wikipedia.org/w/index.php?title=Sport_in_the_Northern_Territory *Contributors*: Chuq, ContiAWB, DjIn, DI2000, Falcadore, Falcon8765, FirefoxRocks, GordyB, Grant65, Hack, InsteadOf, Krabby me, MacRusgail, Mattdocbrown, Numerico, Piano01, Roke, Spy007au, TRS-80, Tabletop, Waacstats, Xfiles82, 9 anonymous edits

Australian rules football in the Northern Territory *Source*: http://en.wikipedia.org/w/index.php?title=Australian_rules_football_in_the_Northern_Territory *Contributors*: AFL Mount Isa, AFL-Cool, Andrwsc, Biatch, DjIn, Gfcpremiers, JPD, Jevansen, JzG, Lindsay658, Moondyne, New World Man, Rulesfan, Spewmaster, The-Pope, Updatehelper, 31 anonymous edits

Tiwi Islands Football League *Source*: http://en.wikipedia.org/w/index.php?title=Tiwi_Islands_Football_League *Contributors*: Biatch, Chuq, Clearwaterlodge, Courcelles, D6, DMacks, DjIn, Footy Freak7, JaGa, Jevansen, Kwamikagami, Michael Hardy, Misarxist, Moondyne, Rogerthat, Rulesfan, Spewmaster, Teddyboy ben, The-Pope, Uncle Dick, WereSpielChequers, Δ, 65 anonymous edits

Tiwi Islands *Source*: http://en.wikipedia.org/w/index.php?title=Tiwi_Islands *Contributors*: Adrian Firth, Angela626, Ashmoo, Biatch, Bidgee, Bimawear, Brynus, Camerong, Chamdarae, Clearwaterlodge, Crusoe8181, DMacks, DaGizza, Dale Arnett, Darwinek, Dinesh smita, Donama, DutchTreat, Epettee, Erebus555, Euryalus, Excirial, Frankie816, Freestyle-69, Gilliam, Gravitone2, Hamiltonstone, Iridescent, JASpencer, JPD, Je suis le tenebreux, Joseph Solis in Australia, Jpatokal, Kanags, Kotuku33, Kwamikagami, Languagegeek, Leuko, Ligulem, Lincolnite, Longhair, Luwilt, Maias, Materialscientist, Michael Glass, Misarxist, Moondyne, Muhandes, Nannus, Noveerbs, Nikai, Nttc, PDH, Paul foord, Piano non troppo, Polyleros, Ratzer, Ricky81, Satrina Brandt, ScottDavis, Shimmeringvibes, Spewmaster, Stephen Bain, Teleomatic, ThujaSol, TristanWhite, 58 anonymous edits

Northern Territory Football League *Source*: http://en.wikipedia.org/w/index.php?title=Northern_Territory_Football_League *Contributors*: Biatch, Bongomanrae, DjIn, Footy Freak7, Hattey, Jeepday, Jellibellee, Jevansen, Longhair, Moondyne, Piano01, Rogerthat, Rulesfan, Saebhiar, Scotty56, Spewmaster, Theshiz162, Tony1, WBardwin, Woohookitty, 88 anonymous edits

AFL Northern Territory *Source*: http://en.wikipedia.org/w/index.php?title=AFL_Northern_Territory *Contributors*: Biatch, DjIn, Longhair, Piano01, Royboycrashfan, Rulesfan, SimonP, 1 anonymous edits

Marrara Stadium *Source*: http://en.wikipedia.org/w/index.php?title=Marrara_Stadium *Contributors*: *Paul*, Aaronrick, AprilHare, AssociateAffiliate, BaldBoris, Bidgee, Bozzio, Chuq, D6, DaGizza, Dale Arnett, Enisternos, Falcadore, Gniina pig warrior, HoldenV8, IPGuGR, Jadr76, Jarrvd95, Jason Recliner Esq., Jonathan Winsky, Kerzaumman, Longhair, MasterMind5001, Mattinbgn, Mattklore, Mendesa, Moondyne, NickelShoe, Patken4, Piano01, Rapturescause, Remy B, Roisterer, Rulesfan, Scotty56, Sem boy, Seth Cohen, Tassedethe, The-Pope, Timmah86, Ukabia, Waacstats, 40 anonymous edits

Traeger Park *Source*: http://en.wikipedia.org/w/index.php?title=Traeger_Park *Contributors*: Aspirex, Biatch, Chuq, D6, DjIn, DI2000, Falcadore, HoldenV8, Jdcooper, Jeff79, Neo Avatars, Piano01, Ramseystreet, Remy B, Rulesfan, Waacstats, 2 anonymous edits

Northern Territory Cricket *Source*: http://en.wikipedia.org/w/index.php?title=Northern_Territory_Cricket *Contributors*: Bill william compton, DjIn, Hack, Hugo999, Sss333, The-Pope, 1 anonymous edits

Rugby league in the Northern Territory *Source*: http://en.wikipedia.org/w/index.php?title=Rugby_league_in_the_Northern_Territory *Contributors*: Angusmclellan, DjIn, GordyB, Jeff79, Rjwilmsi, Saberwyn, 5 anonymous edits

Northern Territory Rugby Union *Source*: http://en.wikipedia.org/w/index.php?title=Northern_Territory_Rugby_Union *Contributors*: DjIn, MacRusgail, SauliH

V8 Supercars *Source*: http://en.wikipedia.org/w/index.php?title=V8_Supercars *Contributors*: 1dragon, 89Fresh, A340-313X, Aflumpire, Alansohn, Alex Destructive, Angusmclellan, Apterygial, Ary29, AtomicSpoon, B3nji, Baggers89, Ballchef, Bart-16, Bearcat, Beaver, Becca888, Ben Ben, BenVic, BengtsonJ, Bggoldie, Bidgee, BigFatBuddha, Billy Liakopoulos, Birky21, Bjthegreat, Bjw 007, Blakeb155, Bongomanrae, Bongwarrior, Breno, Brutaldeluxe, Buckner 1986, CJ, Canterbury Tail, Carrera88, Cheebung, ChicosBailBonds, Chuggwakd, Clown666, Cmdrjameson, Computerjoe, Craigantill, Cs-wolves, Ctbolt, DH85868993, Daniel Guardian, David Waters, Dazdogs, Dbo789, DeafCom, Diceman, Dino246, Dirk kempen, Dogaroon, Draffa, Driftingpuke1, Drmies, Dunc 009, DuncanHill, Dyspepsion, EeepEeep, Ellmist, Enviroboy, Exalt4korn, F1 power, FG42, FPV F6 TYPHOON, Falcadore, Fastford, Fclass, Fcuknzfrenchiracing, Felipe78felipe, FormulaOneFan4Eva, Fredrik, Fruv, FstrthnU, GK1, GTHO, Gaius Cornelius, Gammon, Gene Nygaard, Ghewgill, Ghoongta, Glennobrien, Gnachin, Gparker, Greg the White Falcon, Gregkocook, Grey Shadow, Grover9, Gurch, Hdthanh, Heather.dylan, HexaChord, HoldenSaregreat, HorsePunchKid, Howcheng, Ian Pitchford, ImcdnzI, Impala2009, Inter net, Iohannes Animosus, Ixfd64, JCam, JRA WestyQld2, Jackswill, Jahann37, James086, JamesHoadley, Jdt55, Jeff 8, Jeff79, Jefjeriofjer, Jeremy Visser, JimVC3, Jncraton, John Nevard, John of Reading, Johnmc, John roberts, JonathanDP81, Kass51, Kbdank71, Keenan.hancock, Kennedi, Kevin B12, Killiondude, Kjlewis, Kudz75, Kytabu, LarryGilbert, Liftarn, Lightmouse, Longhair, Lontje, Luigi7, M Johnson, MER-C, Mad maper, Maias, Marek69, Martarius, Matilda, Matthas, Matthew kokai, Meeples, Mksce, Monkey5000, Moondyne, MoondyneAWB, Morio, Morven, Mr Larrington, Mr Moo, Muitint78, Murph fan51, Mwyres, NJM2010, NaBUru38, Neutrality, Nick carson, NigelPorter, Nkid, Norrgard, Nufy8, Officially Mr X, Omicronpersei8, Oromei, Paul foord, Pc13, Penguinboy, Peripitus, Peter Ellis, Piano non troppo, Popsracer, Prisonermonkeys, Prolog, Punctured, R'n'B, RX8I.UVR, Racedriver14, RazorICE, Razzie954, Recury, Reedy, Rich Farmbrough, Rjwilmsi, Robert Fraser, Robert Merkel, Robomaeyhem, Rodeime, RoII, RoryReloaded, Royalbroil, RpgCyco, Ryan john sutton, Sam Blacketer, Scott Paeth, ScottDavis, Seano1, Secfan, Secret Squirrel, Sentry459, Seth Cohen, Sfoskett, Shadowjams, Slj, Slon02, Smmf1, SpackoWinston, Squeakles, SteinbDJ, SunCreator, Supersevenn, Susfele, TBustah, TKLM, Tabletop, Tasmanmotorsportlvr, Tdw77, Teiresias84, Tgv8925, The359, Thebgl, Themeparkgc, ThieLsteve, Thomas Larsen, Tiptoety, Tomcha, Tonytjs, Traediras, UnclearWinter, V8 SuperChat, V8fan, V8s not just for boys, Vicmillsy, Vihari1511, Warnester, Watch37264, Wdyoung, Welsh, Wikipampanga, Willirennen, Windymila, Xbgs351, YUL89YYZ, YellowMonkey, ZoFreX, Zzyzx11, , 797 anonymous edits

Skycity Triple Crown *Source*: http://en.wikipedia.org/w/index.php?title=Skycity_Triple_Crown *Contributors*: Angusmclellan, Armbrust, Dolovis, Falcadore, Tassedethe, V8fan

Darwin Football Stadium *Source*: http://en.wikipedia.org/w/index.php?title=Darwin_Football_Stadium *Contributors*: Andrew.cudzilo, BD2412, D6, DH85868993, ElZilcho, Falcadore, HoldenV8, MoondyneAWB, Piano01, Saberwyn, Timsdad, 4 anonymous edits

Football Federation Northern Territory *Source*: http://en.wikipedia.org/w/index.php?title=Football_Federation_Northern_Territory *Contributors*: Albinomonkey, Australian Matt, Boltonfan22, Borgarde, Chuq, Ctbolt, DjIn, Executive.koala, Falcadore, Farsouth, InsteadOf, MS2ger, Rjwilmsi, Sjmorris007, Socceraust, TInTIn, That Guy, From That Show!, The Frederick, WWGB, Yorktownsquire, 18 anonymous edits

North Queensland Fury F.C. *Source*: http://en.wikipedia.org/w/index.php?title=North_Queensland_Fury_F.C. *Contributors*: 16keeper, A18919, AEKAthensFC, Alan Liefting, Andrew.andii, Aspirina, Astonvilla91, Aussieman92, Australian Matt, Auxodium II, Beantwo, Benjamus, Benstown, BnthI, Boddefan2009, Bongomanrae, Boojanum01, Brycey boy., CK10, Calabe1992, Camw, Canley, Chris G, Chris the speller, ChrisTheDude, Chuq, Ck786, Closedmouth, Cloudz679, CommonsDelinker, Cooldandan, Daniel, Darwinek, Deadman0293, Debresser, Delusion23, Denisarona, Devoindahouse, Dipper123, Dj nix, DjIn, Down7ime, ElZilcho, Euroleague, Excellence Of Execution, Footwiks, Geordietorres, Gialloneri, Grant.Alpaugh, Grenleef, Gunner Shot Stopper, Hack, Hackerr13, HoseloverFat, JRA WestyQld2, Jameboy, Jaredwiltshire, Jimmy Pitt, Jimmy692, Johndman, Kingkewell, Lexusuns, LilHelpa, Lucrab, Lukeswagger, MJW 45, Macktheknifeau, Martinkruse, Mattinbgn, Mattwinter, Mattywhewhite, Melbourne.sport, Mentifisto, Mr Hall of England, Mucker86, NRMZ, Nath1991, Nick Hendo, Nqfury, Number 57, Oddharmonic, Orderinchaos 2, Ozcammo, PeeJay2K3, Portillo, RedsUnited, Rexfan2, Schem, Shiftchange, Sillyfolkboy, Sillyhotdog, Sillysims, Simione001, Sir Sputnik, Soccafanatic7, Squilibob, SuperSam,., Terence Gunning, The Frederick, Timsdad, Townsville, UM 049, Voj 2005, Vripepi, Webzone10, Woohookitty, Xfiles82, YellowMonkey, Zombie433, 643 anonymous edits

Sport in Australia *Source*: http://en.wikipedia.org/w/index.php?title=Sport_in_Australia *Contributors*: 1717, A8UDI, AccAct, Acdc rocks, Actuarial disco boy, AdelaideRandel, Adz2452, Afaber012, Aflumpire, Agnte, Ahunt, Alansohn, Alensha, Alex tan, Alistair85, Allmightyduck, Allstarecho, Amorymeltzer, Amplitude101, Andjam, Andrelim1, AndrewBartlett, AndrewHowse, Anna Lincoln, Anonymous the Editor, Antandrus, Arpan20, Artorius, Ashwinosoft, Aspirex, Australiana, AxelBoldt, BRACK66, Backslash Forwardslash, Ballchef, Bento00, Bidgee, Black Kite, Bloodshedder, Bongomanrae, Borgarde, Boy.pockets, Breawycker, Breno, Btoml4, Buddy F, Bumchewedwelloff, C.Fred, CJ, Calsicol, CanadianLinuxUser, Capricorn42, Casper Claiborne, Chowden9000, CeeWhy2, Cgoodwin, Choalbaton, Chodorkovskiy, Chovain, Chrism, Chuq, Ck786, Ckatz, Closedmouth, Coffeecat91, Colonel Tom, Colonies Chris, Cometstyles, CrackDragon, Craig.Scott, Cricketman2774, Csdm, Cuddy Wifter, Cureden, CurranH, Cursive, Cvene64, D, DH85868993, DJBullfrog, Dale Arnett, Dan027, Dan6541, Danelo, DarbyAsh, Daveb, DeadmanPhenom, Denidowi, DerHexer, Devoindahouse, Dffgd, Dibo, Discospinster, Dl2000, Dmmaus, Doulos Christos, Drbrezniev, Dreadstar, Drinkbeerinpubs, Dudesleeper, DuncanHill, Dureo, ESkog, Ed g2s, EdBever, EffGeeBee, Elassint, Elcobbola, Elitism, Elvisandhismagicpelvis, Enigmaman, Epolk, Esperant, Euchiasmus, Evan C, Falcadore, Feinoha, Felix Portier, FetchcommsAWB, Florrie, Fluffernutter, Flyingdics, Fratrep, GSV Ethics Gradient, Gail, Gaius Cornelius, Gary2863, Gdlrobertson, Gilliam, Gnevin, GordyB, GorillaWarfare, Graham87, Grahamec, Grant65, Grey Shadow, Grimey109, Grimgor79, Gurlpower, Gurt Posh, H-jarrbe, HOUZI, HalfShadow, Harro5, Havenchesse, Hawkeye7, HiLo48, Hobartimus, Hu12, Hydrogen Iodide, InsteadOf, Intelligentsium, Interested, Irishguy, J Milburn, J.delanoy, J04n, JCam, JPD, Jack1810, JamesBWatson, Jay Litman, Jcbarr, Jeff3000, Jeff79, Jenks24, Jevansen, John of Reading, Jorcoga, Jordantrew, Joshua, Junglecat, Kazuba, Kbdank71, Kcsboy2010, Keane Wah, Kharker, Kingutd, Kiwichris1709, KkLaffytaffy, Koerja, Krabby me, Kritterhound, Kudos to you, L Kensington, Landon1980, LauraHale, Law, Liface, Lights, LilHelpa, Loputon, Lord Warlock, Lucasrp, Lukeoz, MSchnitzler2000, Magioladitis, Majorclanger, Malinaccier, Marawe, Martin451, Masonkk, Matilda, Mattdocbrown, Matthewterry87, Mattinbgn, Maxiep, MelbourneStar, Meredyth, Metternech, Michaeln, Mike Rosoft, Milesli, Miss Madeline, Ml grug, Mongrel Punt,

Article Sources and Contributors

Monkeyblue, Moondyne, MoondyneAWB, Moore105464, Moreschi, Moriori, Mowsbury, Mr nice guy, Mythpiano, NW's Public Sock, Nabla, NellieBly, Nick Number, Nigelthevagrant, Nihiltres, Nikai, Norwestie, Nutiketaiel, OlEnglish, Oliverbaasch, Orderinchaos 2, Orenburg1, Ozhistory, POds, Pats987, Pcpp, Penguincentral, Pete Davis, Peter phelps, Petiatil, Pfctdayelise, Pharaoh of the Wizards, Phil Boswell, Piano non troppo, Planetstasiak, Pmberry, Portillo, Prester John, Professor marginalia, Quantpole, RL1991, RainbowOfLight, Randwicked, RandySavageFTW, Raven4x4x, Rcsprinter123, Rebecca, ReeseM, Regancy42, Regibox, Registrarmike, Retired username, Rich Farmbrough, Rich257, Rjensen, Rjwilmsi, Robert Merkel, Rockyg123, Rogerthat, Roke, RoyBoy, Rulesfan, Runewiki777, Ryanorulz, Sam Vimes, Schgooda, ScottDavis, Seb az86556, Seleste123, Senibleconext, Sera Black, Serendipitouscontributor, Severa, Shadowjams, Sheeana, Sickec, Silent Billy, Sillyfolkboy, Simba1409, Sjwjoe321, SkerHawx, Skully Collins, Sliat 1981, Slon02, SmartGuy, Snewoc, Soundabuser, Spamkhh, SpecialWindler, Spewmaster, SpikeToronto, Sportelias16, StAnselm, Stephen Turner, Stmlj, Storm Rider, Striker161, Sydney.city.easts, T0m s 1, THEN WHO WAS PHONE?, THUGCHILDz, Tancred, Tango, Tassedethe, Tewapack, Thatguyflint, Thatsgold, The Brain of Morbius, The Thing That Should Not Be, The-Pope, Theinvestigator08, Thewiikione, Tiburon, Tide rolls, Timprice89, TinTin, Tomasthetankengine, Tommyg06, Tpbradbury, Twsherrin, UncleDouggie, Urgeback, Useight, Uwain, Vladislav, Vclaw, Versus22, Vortexrealm, Vranak, Vrenator, Wayne Slam, Weebs, WheelieBinner, Wildkitten1205, Wimt, Winchelsea, Wjemather, Woohookitty, Wtmitchell, Wysprgr2005, Xiaodai, Xtra, Ylem, Yuanchosaan, Zap Rowsdower, Zntrip, Zomno, Zondor, 966 anonymous edits

Northern Territory *Source*: http://en.wikipedia.org/w/index.php?title=Northern_Territory *Contributors*: 137.111.13.xxx, 149AFK, 1717, 203.37.81.xxx, 99of9, Adamm, AdjustShift, Afterwriting, Aguido, Ahkitj, Aillema, Al Silonov, Alandavidson, AlexiusHoratius, Ali@gwc.org.uk, Andres, Andrew Gwilliam, Angela, Angela26, AnnaFrance, Anonymoues, AussieDingo1983, AussieLegend, Australiana, Avala, AxSkov, B, Badagnani, Barend, Barrylb, Barticus88, Bduke, Bearcat, Bellhalla, Bender235, Bentlibrarian, Biatch, Bidgee, Bissinger, Bjenks, Blake the bookbinder, Bobblewik, BrownHairedGirl, Bryan Derksen, Buaidh, CJ, Calebp-w, Camerong, Canley, Cassowary, Cgaaus, Chanheigeorge, Chenzw, Chiken23, Chris SSIE1, Chris j wood, Chris the speller, Chrislk02, Chuckiesdad, Chuq, Civil Engineer III, ClaretAsh, Clarkk, Closeapple, Cocytus, CommonsDelinker, Conny, Conscious, Conversion script, Cromwelll, Crusoe8181, Cs-wolves, Dainamo, Darkieboy236, David Kernow, Dbenbenn, Dcandeto, Deror avi, Dexta99, Dionville, Djultjula, Dl2000, Drpickem, Dureo, Elekhh, Esperant, Evan Robidoux, FastLizard4, Faustbol, Felix Dance, Fikri, Frankie816, Gaius Cornelius, Gaudoine, Genovue, Ggoudswaard, Gimboid13, Gittinsj, Gnangarra, Golbez, Goldfishbutt, GordyB, Graham87, Greg Winterflood, Ground Zero, Guycalledryan, Hallows AG, Harryboyles, Head, Hugo999, Hunanian, Iainloftus, Indescent, Island, J.delanoy, JNW, Jakia, JamesAM, JamesBWatson, Jaunienij, Jayanntrongol, Jaydec, Jimp, Jncraton, John Hill, Jon Harald Søby, Jonathan321, Jorvik, Joseph Solis in Australia, Jpo, Jsolinsky, Jumbuck, Jutherine, Kaare, Kaaveh Ahangar, Knobbly, Lacrimosus, Lainagier, Lee M, Lerdsuwa, Lonexy, Longhair, Luuva, M.O.X, MJCdetroit, MK8, MacTire02, MacedonianBoy, Magister Mathematicae, Mantes, Marco polo, Marek69, Matilda, Mattinbgn, Mav, Maximus Rex, Metternech, MichaelBillington, Mightygunners, Minemyfaceoff, Moggybreath, Morwen, Mr Rhys, MrTree, Muhandes, Mvjs, NSLE, Nachoman-au, Newverbs, Nicholas Weiner, Nihiltres, NoNonsenseHumJock, NuclearWarfare, Nzseries1, Orderinchaos, Originalwana, OwenBlacker, Ozzieboy, PDH, Pancake7, Paralympic, Patrick, Paul foord, Pedro, Pedro Felipe, Peteboro, Pharos, PhilHibbs, Philip Trueman, Piano01, Piece.of.eight, Pineappleism, Pjf, Pne, Polylerus, Possum, Projoh, Psychohug, QazPlm, Quiensabe, Qxz, RFBailey, RainbowOfLight, Ralmin, Randwicked, Rasvanoel, Ratzer, Rebecca, Riana, Richardcavell, Richde, Rjwilmsi, Roisterer, Roke, Ronline, Ruszewski, Saintrain, Sanx, SatuSuro, Seaphoto, Secfan, Shadowjams, Shamstein, Sharonlwatson, Shrigley, Silentproject, Single16+Sections, Sk8a h8a, Snigbrook, Snowdog, Squamate, StAnselm, Stephen Bain, Stevey7788, Tabletop, Tannin, Template namespace initialisation script, The Emirr, Thortful, Thryduulf, Tide rolls, Tim Starling, Tobby72, Tokek, Travis, Alice Springs, Trek011, Trilobite, Triwbe, Urbanuntil 1, Vaffel, Vclaw, Versus22, Viking880, Vinci Liu, Volantares, Vrenator, Wai Hong, Walkerma, Whytecypress, Woftam, Wongm, Woohookitty, Xenophonana, Xfiles82, Xyzzyva, Yamamoto Ichiro, YellowMonkey, Yewenyi, Zamphuor, Zigger, Zoe, Zscout370, Zzyzx11, 342 anonymous edits

Image Sources, Licenses and Contributors

Image:Aboriginal football.jpg *Source*: http://en.wikipedia.org/w/index.php?title=File:Aboriginal_football.jpg *License*: unknown *Contributors*: Cata, Meno25, Spewmaster, TFCforever, 2 anonymous edits

Image:Hidden Valley Raceway.jpg *Source*: http://en.wikipedia.org/w/index.php?title=File:Hidden_Valley_Raceway.jpg *License*: unknown *Contributors*: User:Bidgee

file:Aboriginal_football.jpg *Source*: http://en.wikipedia.org/w/index.php?title=File:Aboriginal_football.jpg *License*: unknown *Contributors*: Cata, Meno25, Spewmaster, TFCforever, 2 anonymous edits

Image:Football at darwin 1943.jpg *Source*: http://en.wikipedia.org/w/index.php?title=File:Football_at_darwin_1943.jpg *License*: unknown *Contributors*: Rulesfan

Image:Traeger Park 4916.jpg *Source*: http://en.wikipedia.org/w/index.php?title=File:Traeger_Park_4916.jpg *License*: unknown *Contributors*: Toursim NT

File:Sports current event.svg *Source*: http://en.wikipedia.org/w/index.php?title=File:Sports_current_event.svg *License*: unknown *Contributors*: Yuma

File:Tiwi Islands Football League logo.jpg *Source*: http://en.wikipedia.org/w/index.php?title=File:Tiwi_Islands_Football_League_logo.jpg *License*: unknown *Contributors*: Quadell, Salavat, Teddyboy ben, TheDJ

File:Flag of Australia.svg *Source*: http://en.wikipedia.org/w/index.php?title=File:Flag_of_Australia.svg *License*: unknown *Contributors*: Anomie, Mifter

Image:Aboriginal_football.jpg *Source*: http://en.wikipedia.org/w/index.php?title=File:Aboriginal_football.jpg *License*: unknown *Contributors*: Cata, Meno25, Spewmaster, TFCforever, 2 anonymous edits

Image:Tiwi Islands.png *Source*: http://en.wikipedia.org/w/index.php?title=File:Tiwi_Islands.png *License*: unknown *Contributors*: Stephen Bain, Telim tor

File:Tiwi Islands car ferry.jpg *Source*: http://en.wikipedia.org/w/index.php?title=File:Tiwi_Islands_car_ferry.jpg *License*: unknown *Contributors*: User:Satrina Brandt

Image:Tiwi island 2631.jpg *Source*: http://en.wikipedia.org/w/index.php?title=File:Tiwi_island_2631.jpg *License*: unknown *Contributors*: Toursim NT

Image:Tiwi church 2642.jpg *Source*: http://en.wikipedia.org/w/index.php?title=File:Tiwi_church_2642.jpg *License*: unknown *Contributors*: Toursim NT

Image:Carved Poles 2645.jpg *Source*: http://en.wikipedia.org/w/index.php?title=File:Carved_Poles_2645.jpg *License*: unknown *Contributors*: Toursim NT

File:Aboriginal bird carvings.jpg *Source*: http://en.wikipedia.org/w/index.php?title=File:Aboriginal_bird_carvings.jpg *License*: unknown *Contributors*: User:Satrina Brandt

File:Tiwi Island art gallery ceiling.jpg *Source*: http://en.wikipedia.org/w/index.php?title=File:Tiwi_Island_art_gallery_ceiling.jpg *License*: unknown *Contributors*: User:Satrina Brandt

Image:Darwin_Buffaloes_Jumper.svg *Source*: http://en.wikipedia.org/w/index.php?title=File:Darwin_Buffaloes_Jumper.svg *License*: unknown *Contributors*: Saebhiar

Image:Richmond_Tigers_Jumper.svg *Source*: http://en.wikipedia.org/w/index.php?title=File:Richmond_Tigers_Jumper.svg *License*: unknown *Contributors*: Original uploader was Saebhiar at en.wikipedia

Image:Collingwood_Magpies_Jumper.svg *Source*: http://en.wikipedia.org/w/index.php?title=File:Collingwood_Magpies_Jumper.svg *License*: unknown *Contributors*: Original uploader was Saebhiar at en.wikipedia

Image:Southern_Districts_Crocs_Jumper.svg *Source*: http://en.wikipedia.org/w/index.php?title=File:Southern_Districts_Crocs_Jumper.svg *License*: unknown *Contributors*: Saebhiar

Image:St_Marys_Saints_Jumper.svg *Source*: http://en.wikipedia.org/w/index.php?title=File:St_Marys_Saints_Jumper.svg *License*: unknown *Contributors*: Saebhiar

Image:Essendon_Bombers_Jumper.svg *Source*: http://en.wikipedia.org/w/index.php?title=File:Essendon_Bombers_Jumper.svg *License*: unknown *Contributors*: Original uploader was Saebhiar at en.wikipedia

Image:Wanderers_Eagles_Jumper.svg *Source*: http://en.wikipedia.org/w/index.php?title=File:Wanderers_Eagles_Jumper.svg *License*: unknown *Contributors*: Saebhiar

Image:Waratah_Warriors_Jumper.svg *Source*: http://en.wikipedia.org/w/index.php?title=File:Waratah_Warriors_Jumper.svg *License*: unknown *Contributors*: Saebhiar

Image:TIO Stadium.jpg *Source*: http://en.wikipedia.org/w/index.php?title=File:TIO_Stadium.jpg *License*: unknown *Contributors*: User:Bidgee

Image:Ntcricket.PNG *Source*: http://en.wikipedia.org/w/index.php?title=File:Ntcricket.PNG *License*: unknown *Contributors*: Northern Territory Cricket

File:V8 Supercars.svg *Source*: http://en.wikipedia.org/w/index.php?title=File:V8_Supercars.svg *License*: unknown *Contributors*: Avicennasis, Themeparkgc

File:Motorsport current event.svg *Source*: http://en.wikipedia.org/w/index.php?title=File:Motorsport_current_event.svg *License*: unknown *Contributors*: User:Svgalbertian, User:Zzyzx11

Image:V8Supercar-888-Lowndes-2009.jpg *Source*: http://en.wikipedia.org/w/index.php?title=File:V8Supercar-888-Lowndes-2009.jpg *License*: unknown *Contributors*: Blechos

Image:Tander at L&H 500 2008.jpg *Source*: http://en.wikipedia.org/w/index.php?title=File:Tander_at_L&H_500_2008.jpg *License*: unknown *Contributors*: Kytabu

Image:V8 Safety Car.jpg *Source*: http://en.wikipedia.org/w/index.php?title=File:V8_Safety_Car.jpg *License*: unknown *Contributors*: User:Bidgee

Image:2008 Clipsal 500 Podium.jpg *Source*: http://en.wikipedia.org/w/index.php?title=File:2008_Clipsal_500_Podium.jpg *License*: unknown *Contributors*: Ryan Schembri / OzRacingWrap

File:Flag of New South Wales.svg *Source*: http://en.wikipedia.org/w/index.php?title=File:Flag_of_New_South_Wales.svg *License*: unknown *Contributors*: Denelson83, User:Greentubing

File:Flag of Tasmania.svg *Source*: http://en.wikipedia.org/w/index.php?title=File:Flag_of_Tasmania.svg *License*: unknown *Contributors*: User:Denelson83

File:Flag of Queensland.svg *Source*: http://en.wikipedia.org/w/index.php?title=File:Flag_of_Queensland.svg *License*: unknown *Contributors*: User:Denelson83

File:Flag of Victoria (Australia).svg *Source*: http://en.wikipedia.org/w/index.php?title=File:Flag_of_Victoria_(Australia).svg *License*: unknown *Contributors*: User:Denelson83, User:Greentubing

File:Flag of Canada.svg *Source*: http://en.wikipedia.org/w/index.php?title=File:Flag_of_Canada.svg *License*: unknown *Contributors*: Anomie

File:Flag of South Australia.svg *Source*: http://en.wikipedia.org/w/index.php?title=File:Flag_of_South_Australia.svg *License*: unknown *Contributors*: User:Denelson83

File:Flag of New Zealand.svg *Source*: http://en.wikipedia.org/w/index.php?title=File:Flag_of_New_Zealand.svg *License*: unknown *Contributors*: Adambro, Arria Belli, Avenue, Bawolff, Bjankuloski06en, ButterStick, Denelson83, Donk, Duduziq, EugeneZelenko, Fred J, Fry1989, Hugh Jass, Ibagli, Jusjih, Klemen Kocjancic, Mamndassan, Mattes, Nightstallion, O, Peeperman, Poromiami, Reisio, Rfc1394, Shizhao, Tabasco, Transparent Blue, Väsk, Xufanc, Zscout370, 35 anonymous edits

File:Flag of Western Australia.svg *Source*: http://en.wikipedia.org/w/index.php?title=File:Flag_of_Western_Australia.svg *License*: unknown *Contributors*: User:Denelson83

File:North Queensland Fury.svg *Source*: http://en.wikipedia.org/w/index.php?title=File:North_Queensland_Fury.svg *License*: unknown *Contributors*: Avicennasis, Dj nix, Koavf

File:Flag of the Czech Republic.svg *Source*: http://en.wikipedia.org/w/index.php?title=File:Flag_of_the_Czech_Republic.svg *License*: unknown *Contributors*: special commission (of code): SVG version by cs:-xfi-. Colors according to Appendix No. 3 of czech legal Act 3/1993. cs:Zirland.

File:Flag of Papua New Guinea.svg *Source*: http://en.wikipedia.org/w/index.php?title=File:Flag_of_Papua_New_Guinea.svg *License*: unknown *Contributors*: User:Nightstallion

File:Flag of Singapore.svg *Source*: http://en.wikipedia.org/w/index.php?title=File:Flag_of_Singapore.svg *License*: unknown *Contributors*: Various

File:Flag of England.svg *Source*: http://en.wikipedia.org/w/index.php?title=File:Flag_of_England.svg *License*: unknown *Contributors*: Anomie

File:Flag of Uganda.svg *Source*: http://en.wikipedia.org/w/index.php?title=File:Flag_of_Uganda.svg *License*: unknown *Contributors*: User:Nightstallion

File:Flag of Germany.svg *Source*: http://en.wikipedia.org/w/index.php?title=File:Flag_of_Germany.svg *License*: unknown *Contributors*: Anomie

File:Flag of Togo.svg *Source*: http://en.wikipedia.org/w/index.php?title=File:Flag_of_Togo.svg *License*: unknown *Contributors*: Aaker, Ahsoous, EugeneZelenko, Fry1989, Homo lupus, Klemen Kocjancic, Mattes, Mxn, Neq00, Nightstallion, Reisio, ThomasPusch, Vzb83

File:Flag of the Northern Territory.svg *Source*: http://en.wikipedia.org/w/index.php?title=File:Flag_of_the_Northern_Territory.svg *License*: unknown *Contributors*: User:Froztbyte

File:Bondi at sunrise1.jpg *Source*: http://en.wikipedia.org/w/index.php?title=File:Bondi_at_sunrise1.jpg *License*: unknown *Contributors*: Beao, Corevette, Diegotrazzi

File:StateLibQld 1 130135 Cricket players, ca. 1881.jpg *Source*: http://en.wikipedia.org/w/index.php?title=File:StateLibQld_1_130135_Cricket_players,_ca._1881.jpg *License*: unknown *Contributors*:

File:Australia vs England at Adelaide Oval in 1902.jpg *Source*: http://en.wikipedia.org/w/index.php?title=File:Australia_vs_England_at_Adelaide_Oval_in_1902.jpg *License*: unknown *Contributors*: State Library of South Australia

File:StateLibQld 1 120028 Start of the first McDonnell and East foot race from East Brisbane to Tingalpa, 1909.jpg *Source*: http://en.wikipedia.org/w/index.php?title=File:StateLibQld_1_120028_Start_of_the_first_McDonnell_and_East_foot_race_from_East_Brisbane_to_Tingalpa,_1909.jpg *License*: unknown *Contributors*:

File:StateLibQld 1 292827 Group of tennis players, ca. 1922.jpg *Source*: http://en.wikipedia.org/w/index.php?title=File:StateLibQld_1_292827_Group_of_tennis_players,_ca._1922.jpg *License*: unknown *Contributors*: Mattinbgn, Slick

Image Sources, Licenses and Contributors

Image:beach cricket.jpg *Source*: http://en.wikipedia.org/w/index.php?title=File:Beach_cricket.jpg *License*: unknown *Contributors*: laneylou

Image:Telstra Dome wing.jpg *Source*: http://en.wikipedia.org/w/index.php?title=File:Telstra_Dome_wing.jpg *License*: unknown *Contributors*: Original uploader was Carls12 at en.wikipedia

Image:Nblcage.JPG *Source*: http://en.wikipedia.org/w/index.php?title=File:Nblcage.JPG *License*: unknown *Contributors*: Sliat 1981 at en.wikipedia

Image:Ausopen margaret court arena medium.jpg *Source*: http://en.wikipedia.org/w/index.php?title=File:Ausopen_margaret_court_arena_medium.jpg *License*: unknown *Contributors*: FoeNyx, Ivan, Kjetil r, KnowIG, Spyder Monkey

File:2KY (Sky Sports Radio).jpg *Source*: http://en.wikipedia.org/w/index.php?title=File:2KY_(Sky_Sports_Radio).jpg *License*: unknown *Contributors*: The Strikester, Theleftorium

Image:Bobridge, meares and kelly.jpg *Source*: http://en.wikipedia.org/w/index.php?title=File:Bobridge,_meares_and_kelly.jpg *License*: unknown *Contributors*: Blnguyen/

File:Australia v England netball 2008.jpg *Source*: http://en.wikipedia.org/w/index.php?title=File:Australia_v_England_netball_2008.jpg *License*: unknown *Contributors*: paddynapper

File:16 ACPS Atlanta 1996 Australian Swim Team Training.jpg *Source*: http://en.wikipedia.org/w/index.php?title=File:16_ACPS_Atlanta_1996_Australian_Swim_Team_Training.jpg *License*: unknown *Contributors*: GeorgHH, John Vandenberg, Tony.naar

Image:Flag of the Northern Territory.svg *Source*: http://en.wikipedia.org/w/index.php?title=File:Flag_of_the_Northern_Territory.svg *License*: unknown *Contributors*: User:Froztbyte

Image:Tigris-Australia location Northern Territory.svg *Source*: http://en.wikipedia.org/w/index.php?title=File:Tigris-Australia_location_Northern_Territory.svg *License*: unknown *Contributors*: Bidgee, Los688, The Emirr

File:Thomas Baines, Thomas Baines with Aborigines near the mouth of the Victoria River, N.T, 1857.jpg *Source*: http://en.wikipedia.org/w/index.php?title=File:Thomas_Baines,_Thomas_Baines_with_Aborigines_near_the_mouth_of_the_Victoria_River,_N.T,_1857.jpg *License*: unknown *Contributors*: Jacklee, JackyR

Image:Letters Patent Northern Territory.jpg *Source*: http://en.wikipedia.org/w/index.php?title=File:Letters_Patent_Northern_Territory.jpg *License*: unknown *Contributors*: Innotata, PDH, Stefan2

Image:NTRoads.png *Source*: http://en.wikipedia.org/w/index.php?title=File:NTRoads.png *License*: unknown *Contributors*: Original uploader was Fikri at en.wikipedia Later version(s) were uploaded by Clarkk, Mark, Bidgee, Rom rulz424 at en.wikipedia.

Image:Mount Sonder.JPG *Source*: http://en.wikipedia.org/w/index.php?title=File:Mount_Sonder.JPG *License*: unknown *Contributors*: Felix Dance, Nachcommonsverschieber, RedWolf

Image:Kakadu 2488.jpg *Source*: http://en.wikipedia.org/w/index.php?title=File:Kakadu_2488.jpg *License*: unknown *Contributors*: Toursim NT

Image:Uluru NT Australia.JPG *Source*: http://en.wikipedia.org/w/index.php?title=File:Uluru_NT_Australia.JPG *License*: unknown *Contributors*: User:Bo-deh

Image:Fires in Northern Territory, Australia.jpg *Source*: http://en.wikipedia.org/w/index.php?title=File:Fires_in_Northern_Territory,_Australia.jpg *License*: unknown *Contributors*: Jeff Schmaltz

File:Northern Territory Legislative Assembly.jpg *Source*: http://en.wikipedia.org/w/index.php?title=File:Northern_Territory_Legislative_Assembly.jpg *License*: unknown *Contributors*: kenhodge13

Image:Darwin 1993.jpg *Source*: http://en.wikipedia.org/w/index.php?title=File:Darwin_1993.jpg *License*: unknown *Contributors*: Toursim NT

Image:CDU library, Casuarina.jpg *Source*: http://en.wikipedia.org/w/index.php?title=File:CDU_library,_Casuarina.jpg *License*: unknown *Contributors*: Stephen Barnett from Darwin, Australia

Image:Ranger Uranium Mine in Kakadu National Park.jpeg *Source*: http://en.wikipedia.org/w/index.php?title=File:Ranger_Uranium_Mine_in_Kakadu_National_Park.jpeg *License*: unknown *Contributors*: Al Silonov, Hydrargyrum, Ingolfson, Komencanto, Mattinbgn, Teofilo, Vonvon

Image:LasseterHighway.JPG *Source*: http://en.wikipedia.org/w/index.php?title=File:LasseterHighway.JPG *License*: unknown *Contributors*: User:99of9

Image:Ghan at Alice Springs.jpg *Source*: http://en.wikipedia.org/w/index.php?title=File:Ghan_at_Alice_Springs.jpg *License*: unknown *Contributors*: User:WikiWookie

GNU Free Documentation License Version 1.2, November 2002 Copyright (C) 2000,2001,2002 Free Software Foundation, Inc. 59 Temple Place, Suite 330, Boston, MA 02111-1307 USA Everyone is permitted to copy and distribute verbatim copies of this license document, but changing it is not allowed.

0. PREAMBLE

The purpose of this License is to make a manual, textbook, or other functional and useful document "free" in the sense of freedom: to assure everyone the effective freedom to copy and redistribute it, with or without modifying it, either commercially or noncommercially. Secondarily, this License preserves for the author and publisher a way to get credit for their work, while not being considered responsible for modifications made by others. This License is a kind of "copyleft", which means that derivative works of the document must themselves be free in the same sense. It complements the GNU General Public License, which is a copyleft license designed for free software. We have designed this License in order to use it for manuals for free software, because free software needs free documentation: a free program should come with manuals providing the same freedoms that the software does. But this License is not limited to software manuals; [illegible] or whether it is published as a printed book. We recommend this License principally for works whose purpose is instruction or reference.

1. APPLICABILITY AND DEFINITIONS

This License applies to any manual or other work, in any medium, that contains a notice placed by the copyright holder saying it can be distributed under the terms of this License. Such a notice grants a world-wide, royalty-free license, unlimited in duration, to use that work under the conditions stated herein. The "Document", below, refers to any such manual or work. Any member of the public is a licensee, and is addressed as "you". You accept the license if you copy, modify or distribute the work in a way requiring permission under copyright law. A "Modified Version" of the Document means any work containing the Document or a portion of it, either copied verbatim, or with modifications and/or translated into another language. A "Secondary Section" is a named appendix or a front-matter section of the Document that deals exclusively with the relationship of the publishers or authors of the Document to the Document's overall subject (or to related matters) and contains nothing that could fall directly within that overall subject. (Thus, if the Document is in part a textbook of mathematics, a Secondary Section may not explain any mathematics.) The relationship could be a matter of historical connection with the subject or with related matters, or of legal, commercial, philosophical, ethical or political position regarding them. The "Invariant Sections" are certain Secondary Sections whose titles are designated, as being those of Invariant Sections, in the notice that says that the Document is released under this License. If a section does not fit the above definition of Secondary then it is not allowed to be designated as Invariant. The Document may contain zero Invariant Sections. If the Document does not identify any Invariant Sections then there are none. The "Cover Texts" are certain short passages of text that are listed, as Front-Cover Texts or Back-Cover Texts, in the notice that says that the Document is released under this License. A Front-Cover Text may be at most 5 words, and a Back-Cover Text may be at most 25 words. A "Transparent" copy of the Document means a machine-readable copy, represented in a format whose specification is available to the general public, that is suitable for revising the document straightforwardly with generic text editors or (for images composed of pixels) generic paint programs or (for drawings) some widely available drawing editor, and that is suitable for input to text formatters or for automatic translation to a variety of formats suitable for input to text formatters. A copy made in an otherwise Transparent file format whose markup, or absence of markup, has been arranged to thwart or discourage subsequent modification by readers is not Transparent. An image format is not Transparent if used for any substantial amount of text. A copy that is not "Transparent" is called "Opaque". Examples of suitable formats for Transparent copies include plain ASCII without markup, Texinfo input format, LaTeX input format, SGML or XML using a publicly available DTD, and standard-conforming simple HTML, PostScript or PDF designed for human modification. Examples of transparent image formats include PNG, XCF and JPG. Opaque formats include proprietary formats that can be read and edited only by proprietary word processors, SGML or XML for which the DTD and/or processing tools are not generally available, and the machine-generated HTML, PostScript or PDF produced by some word processors for output purposes only. The "Title Page" means, for a printed book, the title page itself, plus such following pages as are needed to hold, legibly, the material this License requires to appear in the title page. For works in formats which do not have any title page as such, "Title Page" means the text near the most prominent appearance of the work's title, preceding the beginning of the body of the text. A section "Entitled XYZ" means a named subunit of the Document whose title either is precisely XYZ or contains XYZ in parentheses following text that translates XYZ in another language. (Here XYZ stands for a specific section name mentioned below, such as "Acknowledgements", "Dedications", "Endorsements", or "History".) To "Preserve the Title" of such a section when you modify the Document means that it remains a section "Entitled XYZ" according to this definition. The Document may include Warranty Disclaimers next to the notice which states that this License applies to the Document. These Warranty Disclaimers are considered to be included by reference in this License, but only as regards disclaiming warranties: any other implication that these Warranty Disclaimers may have is void and has no effect on the meaning of this License.

2. VERBATIM COPYING

You may copy and distribute the Document in any medium, either commercially or noncommercially, provided that this License, the copyright notices, and the license notice saying this License applies to the Document are reproduced in all copies, and that you add no other conditions whatsoever to those of this License. You may not use technical measures to obstruct or control the reading or further copying of the copies you make or distribute. However, you may accept compensation in exchange for copies. If you distribute a large enough number of copies you must also follow the conditions in section 3. You may also lend copies, under the same conditions stated above, and you may publicly display copies.

3. COPYING IN QUANTITY

If you publish printed copies (or copies in media that commonly have printed covers) of the Document, numbering more than 100, and the Document's license notice requires Cover Texts, you must enclose the copies in covers that carry, clearly and legibly, all these Cover Texts: Front-Cover Texts on the front cover, and Back-Cover Texts on the back cover. Both covers must also clearly and legibly identify you as the publisher of these copies. The front cover must present the full title with all words of the title equally prominent and visible. You may add other material on the covers in addition. Copying with changes limited to the covers, as long as they preserve the title of the Document and satisfy these conditions, can be treated as verbatim copying in other respects. If the required texts for either cover are too voluminous to fit legibly, you should put the first ones listed (as many as fit reasonably) on the actual cover, and continue the rest onto adjacent pages. If you publish or distribute Opaque copies of the Document numbering more than 100, you must either include a machine-readable Transparent copy along with each Opaque copy, or state in or with each Opaque copy a computer-network location from which the general network-using public has access to download using public-standard network protocols a complete Transparent copy of the Document, free of added material. If you use the latter option, you must take reasonably prudent steps, when you begin distribution of Opaque copies in quantity, to ensure that this Transparent copy will remain thus accessible at the stated location until at least one year after the last time you distribute an Opaque copy (directly or through your agents or retailers) of that edition to the public. It is requested, but not required, that you contact the authors of the Document well before redistributing any large number of copies, to give them a chance to provide you with an updated version of the Document.

4. MODIFICATIONS

You may copy and distribute a Modified Version of the Document under the conditions of sections 2 and 3 above, provided that you release the Modified Version under precisely this License, with the Modified Version filling the role of the Document, thus licensing distribution and modification of the Modified Version to whoever possesses a copy of it. In addition, you must do these things in the Modified Version: A. Use in the Title Page (and on the covers, if any) a title distinct from that of the Document, and from those of previous versions (which should, if there were any, be listed in the History section of the Document). You may use the same title as a previous version if the original publisher of that version gives permission. B. List on the Title Page, as authors, one or more persons or entities responsible for authorship of the modifications in the Modified Version, together with at least five of the principal authors of the Document (all of its principal authors, if it has fewer than five), unless they release you from this requirement. C. State on the Title page the name of the publisher of the Modified Version, as the publisher. D. Preserve all the copyright notices of the Document. E. Add an appropriate copyright notice for your modifications adjacent to the other copyright notices. F. Include, immediately after the copyright notices, a license notice giving the public permission to use the Modified Version under the terms of this License, in the form shown in the Addendum below. G. Preserve in that license notice the full lists of Invariant Sections and required Cover Texts given in the Document's license notice. H. Include an unaltered copy of this License. I. Preserve the section Entitled "History", Preserve its Title, and add to it an item stating at least the title, year, new authors, and publisher of the Modified Version as given on the Title Page. If there is no section Entitled "History" in the Document, create one stating the title, year, authors, and publisher of the Document as given on its Title Page, then add an item describing the Modified Version as stated in the previous sentence. J. Preserve the network location, if any, given in the Document for public access to a Transparent copy of the Document, and likewise the network locations given in the Document for previous versions it was based on. These may be placed in the "History" section. You may omit a network location for a work that was published at least four years before the Document itself, or if the original publisher of the version it refers to gives permission. K. For any section Entitled "Acknowledgements" or "Dedications", Preserve the Title of the section, and preserve in the section all the substance and tone of each of the contributor acknowledgements and/or dedications given therein. L. Preserve all the Invariant Sections of the Document, unaltered in their text and in their titles. Section numbers or the equivalent are not considered part of the section titles. M. Delete any section Entitled "Endorsements". Such a section may not be included in the Modified Version. N. Do not retitle any existing section to be Entitled "Endorsements" or to conflict in title with any Invariant Section. O. Preserve any Warranty Disclaimers. If the Modified Version includes new front-matter sections or appendices that qualify as Secondary Sections and contain no material copied from the Document, you may at your option designate some or all of these sections as invariant. To do this, add their titles to the list of Invariant Sections in the Modified Version's license notice. These titles must be distinct from any other section titles. You may add a section Entitled "Endorsements", provided it contains nothing but endorsements of your Modified Version by various parties--for example, statements of peer review or that the text has been approved by an organization as the authoritative definition of a standard. You may add a passage of up to five words as a Front-Cover Text, and a passage of up to 25 words as a Back-Cover Text, to the end of the list of Cover Texts in the Modified Version. Only one passage of Front-Cover Text and one of Back-Cover Text may be added by (or through arrangements made by) any one entity. If the Document already includes a cover text for the same cover, previously added by you or by arrangement made by the same entity you are acting on behalf of, you may not add another; but you may replace the old one, on explicit permission from the previous publisher that added the old one. The author(s) and publisher(s) of the Document do not by this License give permission to use their names for publicity for or to assert or imply endorsement of any Modified Version.

5. COMBINING DOCUMENTS

You may combine the Document with other documents released under this License, under the terms defined in section 4 above for modified versions, provided that you include in the combination all of the Invariant Sections of all of the original documents, unmodified, and list them all as Invariant Sections of your combined work in its license notice, and that you preserve all their Warranty Disclaimers. The combined work need only contain one copy of this License, and multiple identical Invariant Sections may be replaced with a single copy. If there are multiple Invariant Sections with the same name but different contents, make the title of each such section unique by adding at the end of it, in parentheses, the name of the original author or publisher of that section if known, or else a unique number. Make the same adjustment to the section titles in the list of Invariant Sections in the license notice of the combined work. In the combination, you must combine any sections Entitled "History" in the various original documents, forming one section Entitled "History"; likewise combine any sections Entitled "Acknowledgements", and any sections Entitled "Dedications". You must delete all sections Entitled "Endorsements".

6. COLLECTIONS OF DOCUMENTS

You may make a collection consisting of the Document and other documents released under this License, and replace the individual copies of this License in the various documents with a single copy that is included in the collection, provided that you follow the rules of this License for verbatim copying of each of the documents in all other respects. You may extract a single document from such a collection, and distribute it individually under this License, provided you insert a copy of this License into the extracted document, and follow this License in all other respects regarding verbatim copying of that document.

7. AGGREGATION WITH INDEPENDENT WORKS

A compilation of the Document or its derivatives with other separate and independent documents or works, in or on a volume of a storage or distribution medium, is called an "aggregate" if the copyright resulting from the compilation is not used to limit the legal rights of the compilation's users beyond what the individual works permit. When the Document is included in an aggregate, this License does not apply to the other works in the aggregate which are not themselves derivative works of the Document. If the Cover Text requirement of section 3 is applicable to these copies of the Document, then if the Document is less than one half of the entire aggregate, the Document's Cover Texts may be placed on covers that bracket the Document within the aggregate, or the electronic equivalent of covers if the Document is in electronic form. Otherwise they must appear on printed covers that bracket the whole aggregate.

8. TRANSLATION

Translation is considered a kind of modification, so you may distribute translations of the Document under the terms of section 4. Replacing Invariant Sections with translations requires special permission from their copyright holders, but you may include translations of some or all Invariant Sections in addition to the original versions of these Invariant Sections. You may include a translation of this License, and all the license notices in the Document, and any Warranty Disclaimers, provided that you also include the original English version of this License and the original versions of those notices and disclaimers. In case of a disagreement between the translation and the original version of this License or a notice or disclaimer, the original version will prevail. If a section in the Document is Entitled "Acknowledgements", "Dedications", or "History", the requirement (section 4) to Preserve its Title (section 1) will typically require changing the actual title.

9. TERMINATION

You may not copy, modify, sublicense, or distribute the Document except as expressly provided for under this License. Any other attempt to copy, modify, sublicense or distribute the Document is void, and will automatically terminate your rights under this License. However, parties who have received copies, or rights, from you under this License will not have their licenses terminated so long as such parties remain in full compliance.

10. FUTURE REVISIONS OF THIS LICENSE

The Free Software Foundation may publish new, revised versions of the GNU Free Documentation License from time to time. Such new versions will be similar in spirit to the present version, but may differ in detail to address new problems or concerns. See http://www.gnu.org/copyleft/. Each version of the License is given a distinguishing version number. If the Document specifies that a particular numbered version of this License "or any later version" applies to it, you have the option of following the terms and conditions either of that specified version or of any later version that has been published (not as a draft) by the Free Software Foundation. If the Document does not specify a version number of this License, you may choose any version ever published (not as a draft) by the Free Software Foundation. ADDENDUM: How to use this License for your documents To use this License in a document you have written, include a copy of the License in the document and put the following copyright and license notices just after the title page: Copyright (c) YEAR YOUR NAME. Permission is granted to copy, distribute and/or modify this document under the terms of the GNU Free Documentation License, Version 1.2 or any later version published by the Free Software Foundation; with no Invariant Sections, no Front-Cover Texts, and no Back-Cover Texts. A copy of the license is included in the section entitled "GNU Free Documentation License". If you have Invariant Sections, Front-Cover Texts and Back-Cover Texts, replace the "with...Texts." line with this: with the Invariant Sections being LIST THEIR TITLES, with the Front-Cover Texts being LIST, and with the Back-Cover Texts being LIST. If you have Invariant Sections without Cover Texts, or some other combination of the three, merge those two alternatives to suit the situation. If your document contains nontrivial examples of program code, we recommend releasing these examples in parallel under your choice of free software license, such as the GNU General Public License, to permit their use in free software.

Lightning Source UK Ltd.
Milton Keynes UK
UKOW05f0328030813

214801UK00001B/248/P